A Goddess In My Shoes
Seven Steps To Peace

D0973003

A Goddess In My Shoes
Seven Steps To Peace

Rickie Moore

TM

Trade Paperbacks
For the Future . . . And Beyond

HUMANICS NEW AGE
Post Office Box 7447
Atlanta, Georgia 30309

TM

Trade Paperbacks
For the Future . . . And Beyond

HUMANICS NEW AGE
P.O. Box 7447
Atlanta, Georgia 30309

First Printing 1988
Copyright© 1988 Humanics Limited
All rights reserved. No part of this book may be reproduced or used in
any form or by any means — graphic, electronic, or mechanical, including photocopying, recording, taping, or information storage and
retrieval systems — without written permission of the publishers.

PRINTED IN THE UNITED STATES OF AMERICA

Library of Congress Cataloging-in-Publication Data

Moore, Rickie.
    A Goddess in My Shoes: Seven Steps to Peace/Rickie Moore.
      p.   cm.
    Translation of:
    Bibliography: p.
    ISBN 0-89334-109-6
    1. Housewives-Psychology. 2. Spiritual life. 3. Feminism-
    Religious aspects. 4. Goddesses. I. Title.
    HQ1206.M6525 1988
    305.4'2—dc19   88-9243
                                           CIP

This book is dedicated to the goddess in everyone . . . and to my beloved husband, about whom I am speechless.

Contents

Preface

Dear Reader,
I've spent most of my life searching for the same things everyone wants: a lot of love, a few good laughs, and a little peace.

Being a naturally nervous, hard-core worrier, I had to learn tricks to get peaceful. I wanted to live life like a song. It wasn't hard to find teachers touting transcendence, the trick was finding teachers who live the song they sing.

As a daughter, I discovered parents are people I couldn't live with and couldn't leave either. As a mother, I learned that successful parenting meant not having my kids stab me in my sleep. As a wife, I discovered my sexuality was a gateway to God. Shamanic adventures taught me that even healers need to be healed. After surviving discipleship, I realized that *Guru* means, "Gee, you are you." Practicing yoga taught me to never underestimate a disciplined person who can stand on one leg as easily as two. Being a therapist helped me see that holy people are just ordinary human beings coming close to their potential, and that people are perfect . . . it's the world that's crazy.

A Goddess In My Shoes celebrates the universality of the human struggle, and because I only know what I've lived, it focuses on my personal search for truth, freedom, and a good bowl of spaghetti. Nobody's life is private. There are no secrets . . . we just wish there were. I share the lessons I've learned from the great classroom of life, hoping they prove useful to you in creating your own special and unique lessons.

On one level *A Goddess In My Shoes* is an entertainment providing laughter, tears, counsel, even a sense of belonging. On another level it offers some special yogic/shamanic/energetic exercises that have helped me stay sane in a crazy world. It describes the effect life has on our chakras . . . and how, as we go up the chakras, we change our lives.

If you open your heart and experience the love with which this book was written, and if you drop your prejudices and beliefs, you will have done the most important exercise of this book. I don't promise you'll be released from the burdens of your past, or freed from the dangers we face in the future, but perhaps when the hurdles are highest and the only reason you have for feeling grateful is that you don't have to eat a live frog, you'll feel peaceful knowing that we can take ourselves a little less seriously and rejoice in the miracle of being human.

Rickie Moore

Acknowledgments

I am grateful to Steven Fenberg, Mariann & Bernhard Leuthold-Thonen, Petra & Martin Boss, Christa & Hubert Alf, Henrietta & Roberto Preinreich, Michael Harlacher, Koos Oeberius Kaptijn, Christel & Eleonore & Will Kluth, Ronya Brokbals, Thea Brokke-de Jager, Jutta Hartel, Leona Kellerman, Christian Rieder, Ingrid Hubjer, Nico & Ariet Vissel, Marianne Knecht, Elisabeth Hilbeg, Aaron Lowery, and Wicca.

I would like to acknowledge the inspiration from the stars in the eyes of Shiloh, Albert Hofmann, Elbert Hubbard, Hazel Stanley, Danny Slomoff, Charles Muir, Joel Edelman, Bob Schaibly, Elise Orman, Satya, Sadhu Singh Khalsa, Don Snell, Alberto Villoldo, Don Eduardo Caldedron, Paul Soderburg, Don Bushnell, Don Jose, Yogi Bhajan, Paul Kluwer, Adano Ley, Sant Keshavadas and . . . Charlie.

I would like to acknowledge the artistic talents of Cindy Freedman, Loretta Koopmans, Michael Boltz, Sharon Stewart, Ilse Engl, Earl Wilson, Jr., Peter Alsop, Anselm Konig, Gerry Daamen, Carl Sagan, and Robert Freedman. I want to thank Paul Peacock for the illustrations in this book.

Nothing would have been possible without the love and trust of my two daughters, Rhonda and Lauren, and of each person who has attended workshops . . . the family.

Introduction

If we want to be peaceful and go from surviving to thriving, it helps to know what we're afraid of. We humans are afraid of the unknown. So, if we don't know ourselves, we are naturally afraid of who we are. Since fear and peace mix about as well as politics and truth, it's logical that to be peaceful, we have to know ourselves. But there are as many ways to get to know ourselves as there are selves to get to know. The good news is that once we get to know ourselves we begin to accept the things we wanted to change . . . and by then we're changed!

A Goddess In My Shoes uses the chakras, the seven vital energy centers in the human being, as a map to explore who we are, how we got the way we are, and what we can do to become who we want to be.

What we humans are, in fact, is energy. We vibrate at various intensities and frequencies. These frequencies are levels of consciousness. In each of us there are seven vital force centers of energy, like spinning wheels of star stuff. Familiarizing ourselves with our chakras, and learning to balance and harmonize them, can provide us with inner peace. Security comes from knowing that we can spin our own energies to design the fabric of our lives. A successful journey up the chakras, up the levels of consciousness, means going from matter to spirit . . . and making spirit matter.

If we divide the seven chakras into lower and upper triads, the lower three (anus, sex organs and solar plexus) are concerned with matter. The upper three (throat, brow center and crown) are related to spirit. The fourth chakra, the heart center, is the pivot point that can provide the balance between matter and spirit.

It requires love to balance our lives and the polarities in ourselves. Some people get stuck at one level of consciousness. A balanced person, however, is one who can consciously choose to put more or less energy into any one of the seven chakras . . . at will.

The first chakra, in the region of the anus and base of the spine, is concerned with survival. This center's elemental quality is earth. People stuck at this material level, with a survival mentality, are over-invested in acquiring things they think they need. Their greed is motivated by a fear of not surviving. Because they believe that more and bigger means better, they often act like assholes. Appropriately, this chakra controls the sense of smell. A balanced first chakra takes little energy . . . it runs on instinct.

The second chakra, the region of the sex organs and spleen, is the home of the libido: the driving life force for procreation, recreation, inspiration and rejuvenation. This center's element is water and its sense is taste. The issues connected with the second chakra are naturally sexual, and are the gateways to heaven and hell. People stuck here are at the mercy of the tides of passion and are often drowned in a flood of loveless lust. They are the universal macho male and femme fatale. A balanced second chakra is the gateway to seventh heaven.

The third chakra, in the region of the solar plexus and belly, is the home of will power and the seat of emotions. Its issues involve the pursuit of personal power, and the need to individuate. A balanced third chakra brings divine will. This center controls sight, and people stuck here are often in a blind rage. Third chakra people might be seen as pushy, aggressive and hot-tempered. The elemental quality is . . . fire.

The fourth chakra, the heart center, is the home of compassion, empathy and love. The element is air. An open heart makes life lighter. A heart that rarely opens . . . often breaks. The heart relates to the sense of touch. No one is untouched by the experience of love, or the lack of it. An open-hearted person can heal with loving touch.

The fifth chakra, the throat center, is where we generate the power to communicate, commune, share and express ourselves. This center controls the sense of hearing, and its element is ether, from which we derive all sound. When we're in the fifth chakra, we can hear the sounds of silence and know the etheric in ourselves. Fifth chakra people understand that it's more important to understand than to be understood.

The sixth chakra, the brow center at the region of the third eye, houses intuition and controls thoughts. By transmitting and receiving with a sixth sense, we can know the past, present and future. By channeling thought currents, we can influence humanity and create a state of grace. Sixth chakra people are rare.

The seventh chakra, the crown of the head where we see halos depicted, is the haven of enlightenment. However we arrive at the seventh chakra, whether through yoga or sex or drugs or years of solitude and celibacy, and whether we believe in enlightenment or not, we all have the capacity to experience ourselves without ego, without doubt, without thought, without desire . . . if only for an instant. We can, from time-to-time, experience a moment of bliss, a state of grace and all-oneness with all life, and in that instant we come home . . . to seventh heaven. Enlightenment, like the moon, waxes and wanes, comes and goes . . . and there are as many heavens to get to as there are ways to get to heaven. Seventh chakra people are usually crucified, venerated, assassinated or revered.

Although some people never rise above the earth and others get stuck in the clouds, nobody remains in just one chakra all the time. Changes in consciousness are part of life. One way to know where a person is coming from is to know which chakra they're coming from.

Consider an ordinary question an ordinary man might ask his wife, "What do you think dear? Should I take that job in Australia?"

From the first chakra the wife might answer, "What if you don't like it and we have to leave? What if we lose everything and have to start over?" She's worried about survival.

From the second chakra the wife might say with a gleam in her eye, "Well, if it will mean we can have more time in bed, I'm all for it, honey." She's feeling sexy.

From the third chakra the wife might reply, "What about me? Don't I count? What about *my* job?" She's engaged in a power struggle.

From the fourth chakra she might say, "I'll love you whatever you do." She's compassionate and open-hearted.

From the fifth chakra the wife might respond, "I can hear how excited you are about taking that job." She's tuned-in and receptive.

From the sixth she could say, "I know we're going to have a great time in Australia." She's intuitive and knows what's coming.

From the seventh chakra the woman might either smile with such acceptance and delight that she wouldn't have to say anything, or she might say, "Why not?"

If there is a trick to living life like a song, it is simply to learn to play the chakras like musical notes. I share with you my personal struggle for harmony including the sour notes.

Truth is personal, and no two people's lives are the same. By sharing how I managed to harmonize my energies in the context of my life, I hope to inspire you to realize that peace is possible in your life, too. If a bourgeoise housewife like me could find a goddess in her shoes, so can you!

A Goddess In My Shoes

Seven Steps To Peace

RED EARTH SMELL

Location: *anus*

Sound: *LAM*

Color: *red*

Element: *earth*

Function: *survival*

Sense: *smell*

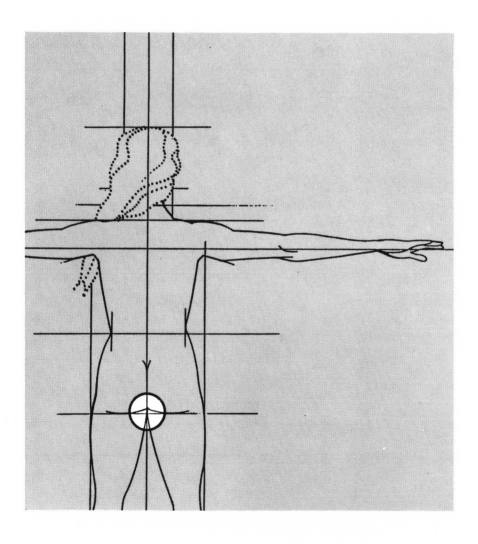

Issues

PHYSIOLOGICAL issues include disorders of the region of the anus and the base of the spine, including the colon . . . constipation, hemorrhoids, diarrhea, colitis. Also included are disorders of solid matter in the body such as bones, teeth and nails. Problems with the sense of smell include no ability to smell and hypersensitivity to odors. Balanced physical functions bring ease to elimination.

EMOTIONAL/BEHAVIORAL issues deal with basic insecurity about surviving. Problems include procrastination, laziness, television addiction, excessive stingyness, greed and worry . . . as well as shopping-itis, bragging, compulsive gambling, daredevil stunts, panic attacks, terror and violent actions. These behaviors may result in a person being called tight-ass, asshole, terrorist. . . . Balanced emotional functioning brings security about being able to survive.

SPIRITUAL issues concern being so grounded that subtle energies are virtually meaningless. Balanced spiritual functioning brings the Kingdom of Heaven to earth.

Questions

- Can I make it?
- What if . . . I fail? What if I succeed?
        . . . I'm alone? What if I can't cope?
        . . . I struggle for nothing?
        . . . I have nothing to struggle for?
        . . . I stay depressed?
        . . . I go crazy?
        . . . I hurt someone?
        . . . nobody wants me?
        . . . I'm rejected or abandoned?
        . . . I die before I live?

Survival

Don't Take Yourself Seriously

No Matter how grave your plight
No difference how great our fright
Irrelevant the severity
Of no interest insecurity
Unimportant is the past
Nobody cares what we did last.
We can laugh at ourselves deliriously
If we don't take ourselves too seriously.

I was an ordinary cosmic law-abiding citizen, looking for some praise and a little peace. I was hoping to learn ways to feel better, safer and happier, but it wasn't possible . . . surviving had become a full-time job. I was worried. Surviving can be a pain in the ass. I was anxious. It's easy to feel anxious. Just one little missile accidentally being fired by a temperamental computer could ruin a person's whole day.

I didn't know who I was and I was afraid if I found out, I wouldn't want to tell anybody. All I'd seen of myself were reflections in distorted mirrors. All I'd ever heard was, "You're too skinny . . . too fat . . . too slow . . . too pretty . . . too dumb . . . too smart . . . too lazy . . . too sexy . . . or too much like Uncle John." I needed my mother's criticism the way a turkey needs Christmas. When I learned people needed a little love and some honest praise to be motivated to survive, I was amazed I ever made it out of bed.

I thought everyone knew more, lived better, had more friends, cleaner toilets, brighter teeth and better sex than I did. Somehow, I managed to feel less important, less worthy, more alone and older than everybody. I was relieved when I discovered most people got the same messages I did and were equally stuffed with criticism and starved for praise. When I began to realize that I wasn't so different from other people, that everyone gets depressed, sad, scared and angry, I was overjoyed. When I learned we all need to be held and loved, or at least liked and listened to, I began to realize I was normal. That was my first group identity: normal. Then surviving picked up. I had a real sense of belonging.

Naturally, after years of being asked "Who do you think you are?" I was a little insecure. I worried about almost everything: not being able to cope; going crazy; trying to survive without a man; being rejected, betrayed, abandoned, depressed; becoming successful; failing; being old and even dying before I really lived. I worried about my children if they stayed out too late, if they came home too early, and if their grades were too high. Boy, was I normal!

I began to see how similar we humans are in our struggles, and how isolated we've been not to have noticed. For example, most people have a fear of betrayal. It's understandable since our first betrayal is usually around four, when we discover that Santa Claus is a fraud. How could a kid trust anybody after that?

My self-esteem had no chance to increase because I married a man who picked up where my parents left off. He was dependent on me to be dependent on him. I wanted to become a therapist and help people find ways to avoid premature death from aggravation. He wanted me to go to cooking school. Despite my fear of rejection, I dragged myself to the school of my choice, only to find I couldn't afford the tuition without his support. I was a poor little rich girl, trapped in a swanky suburban cage. As soon as I saw I was in prison, I began to plan a jail break.

I had two little girls and I was pregnant. After the tragic death of my new-born daughter in the hospital nursery, I was not only unable to stop grieving . . . I was unable to stop bleeding as well. The surgery to stop my bleeding also stopped my heart. During this near-death experience, I got the best messages of my life: after passing through a series of lighted archways I began to hear voices that said I had a purpose in life and it was too soon to die. I came home from the hospital knowing that my life was heading in a new direction.

A few months later I took one last look at the crystal-clear waters of my designer swimming pool, the envy of the neighborhood. Then like Scarlett O'Hara and her carrot, I ceremoniously raised a can of floor wax over my head and dramatically poured it into the pool, vowing to never again wax a kitchen floor. I burned my bra and traded my platinum wig for a French beret. Luckily, survival is instinctive. I took my two children, my dog, and what was left of my spirit, filled my El Camino with my paintings, and drove off with two flat tires.

I had spent years in art school, mostly because they had great coffee in the cafeteria. Now I was determined to earn a living selling the paintings I thought no one would buy. I bought an old house from a woman who believed I would become a successful painter because I wore sandals, that French beret, and said "voila" a lot. I believed the quaint and crooked roof would cooperate and make it until I did. We were both wrong. The roof collapsed during a memorable rain that washed my paintings and my aspirations down the soggy streets.

I took my ordinary, cosmic, law-abiding body and laid it across a psychiatrist's couch. He assured me that given enough time and ample tranquilizers, he could cure me of my anxieties. I watched him cough and absentmindedly put his cigarette out in his candy dish while nervously avoiding eye contact with me. I left with a never-ending prescription for Valium, wondering why he thought I was the only one who needed help.

What to do? About the time I thought I had some answers, the questions changed. I was so nervous I drank coffee just to calm down. I took a good look at myself in a mirror. Some people looked as though their bodies were held up by a coat hanger; mine looked like I'd swallowed one. I used to be the skinniest kid in my neighborhood and nothing had changed. My back was as round as a bowling ball from years of trying to hide my breasts with my shoulders. I knew some anxiety was healthy, it indicates that there's still some brain activity; but I saw the left-over traumas of my childhood lurking in the cells of my body. They weren't just hanging around either. They were waving flags and demanding dues. I knew I needed to let go of some of my stress, or there'd be nothing left to worry about.

My children were supportive of my search for peace. After all, who wants a mother you can only see during visiting hours? They encouraged me to get going . . . even if it was to doctors, lawyers, therapists, bars or singles' socials.

Somehow I found myself going to a kundalini yoga class in an ashram in Texas with a group of turbaned ex-cowboys. Knowing as much about kundalini yoga as I did about the sex life of a crippled chicken, I relaxed and let the teacher take me on the first guided inner journey of my life.

I had done some hatha yoga before, but this kundalini was fast moving, dynamic, demanding and fun! I had no time to think during the session, and consequently felt as though I had been given a ticket . . . good any time . . . to realms of happier consciousness. I was so relaxed at the end of the session that I wasn't afraid to worry about what I was going to do about the rest of my life.

Thank God for Charlie. He's the kind of friend everyone wants. Charlie's smile could melt the snows of Kilimanjaro. I confessed my fears and opened up to him uninhibitedly. When I told him I was worried about rejection, he assured me it was normal and that a few good rejections would cure me. I trusted Charlie. I began to get rejected. Once I found how easy it was, I had no trouble managing a few a week.

Once, I asked a very handsome man in an elevator if he would like to have dinner with me that night. I held my breath, hoping for a quick rejection. Instead, he smiled, took my hand, and offered me a job in his bank.

When I told Charlie I was afraid of going crazy he laughed, "Normal people tend to go crazy when they're separated from nature."

It was my turn to laugh. I was as at home in the woods as a bear is on a bidet.

"People go crazy when they're subjected to over-crowding, politics, and too much television," Charlie said gently.

I visualized five o'clock freeways, politicians and television's relentless demands that I stay young, odorless and skinny.

"People often go crazy just trying to live up to other people's expectations," Charlie said.

I saw images of myself, the veins in my neck thick and purple, as I screamed, strained and begged for approval from just about anybody.

Charlie said, "Let yourself have a good scream, cry, or laugh, and you won't need to go crazy. It's just a way of coping when all else fails."

A few days later, I came home from the dentist's office feeling numb. I discovered my washing machine had developed a mind of its own. The kitchen floor had flooded and my dog managed to slip and break her leg. It was still early enough when I returned home from the veterinarian's with my car burning up, to receive a subpoena from a neighbor who was suing me for playing music I never played, sprain my wrist wrestling with an antique ironing board, and contend with an under-qualified, over-sexed plumber. By the time my kids came home, only my body was walking around . . . my mind had the good sense to leave.

Then I heard, "One good cry beats asking why."

I locked my bedroom door, leaped onto the bed and began hitting, kicking, screaming and crying so loud, my neighbor not only dropped the law suit . . . he offered to pay me to play music.

The relief was so great after my temper tantrum, I couldn't understand why we weren't taught how to do this in school. My kids weren't even allowed to scream on the playground at their school. I protested the policy but I didn't get anywhere. The principal thought I was just another frustrated woman with too much to do.

Charlie was right. I knew after that temper tantrum, that as long as I could cry, scream and laugh, I would never go crazy. But how could I convince my mother? She was sure I was already crazy because only a crazy woman would leave a man who made as much money as my husband did. My daughters assured me I was crazy, because only a crazy lady would give them spaghetti for breakfast.

I decided to teach my daughters how to have a temper tantrum, but they taught me. "Kick harder, Mom!" they laughed. "Scream louder! Let it out!" they encouraged. Together we discovered that the only thing better than a good cry is a great laugh.

Laughing in my mother's house when I was growing up was as taboo as whistling, and was responded to with enormously opened eyes, pointed fingers, and threats of annihilation. Besides, my mother prided herself on her ability to never laugh at anything.

"It's not my fault," I thought one dismal day at the ashram as I battled my body and lost. "I'm a powerless weakling." I was stretching my legs in a yoga posture, but since they hadn't been bent that way in twenty years, they resisted. Touching my toes seemed as remote as winning a gold medal in the Olympics. "I'm just not flexible," I thought, inwardly despising an eighteen-year-old adept sitting in front of me in the yoga class.

A few minutes later, I was standing in a kundalini yoga posture called "archer pose," poised like an archer pulling a bow with my arms. We had to hold the position forever. Actually, it was for nine minutes, but it felt like eternity.

Just before I was about to give up and crumble, I heard, "You just believe you can't do it. . . . Keep up, you can do it. You just believe you're not strong enough, but *you can do it!*"

Suddenly, scenes began to flash before me. I saw myself as an American Indian woman, protecting my family from a charging rhinoceros. Then I saw myself as Joan of Arc, holding off King Kong.

"Ninety seconds," the teacher said.

I saw myself as William Tell, shooting a wormy apple from my son's head.

"Ten seconds," the teacher whispered, and I knew I was home. I could feel a smile breaking out on my face. I only believed I was a weak and delicate flower. I was in fact Hercules, disguised as an ordinary, skinny lady. I really could do it. The pain disappeared and I felt as though I could have held the posture indefinitely.

"Inhale," the teacher said flatly, and I broke through my physical boundaries. I made it! I was free of self-imposed limitations, of debilitating beliefs.

As I lay on the floor of that ashram, on a clean white sheet spread on top of some old grey carpet, listening to an ex-drummer play a great gong, I felt absolute peace. I felt unafraid. My entire belief system evaporated like my perspiration. I felt a sense of security, of self-esteem, and I knew I could cope. I had experienced the wisdom of my body without the interference of my mind.

That night, I made a list of my beliefs and Charlie asked, "Who told you that?" or, "How do you know that?," after each one. By the time we finished, I felt like a naked porcupine, only softer. Every belief kept me from knowing something. Simply believing that I had to shake a pot while popping popcorn, kept me from knowing that you don't have to . . . it pops just fine by itself. Believing that dogs need meat kept me from knowing that vegetarian dogs live as long, and are just as healthy, happy and horny.

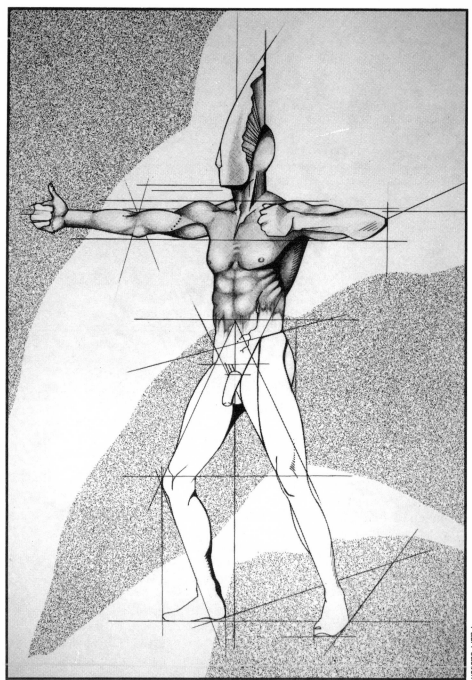

Each belief belonged to someone else. I had always believed what I was taught, and mostly did what I was told. No wonder I sounded like my mother. I actually believed that my mother was always right; that I had to be thin to be loved; that I had to please my parents, husband, and children; that good mothers stayed home; and that if I had a big house, a big car, a big bank account and a big-shot husband, I could get away with having a big mouth.

I believed people were either terrific or turkeys. I believed that myth so completely that I could excommunicate a whole culture with three little words like "Those people lie."

I believed the government was a substitute parent that would protect me when my parents couldn't; that anyone outside of my blood family would turn away in disgust if I needed help; that all women were my competitors and couldn't be trusted; that men only wanted me to "do it" with, and that if I "did it" before I married, everyone would know.

I believed that at twenty-eight, I was too old to change; that no man wants an older woman with two children; and that on my thirtieth birthday I would awaken to find the remains of my once-sexy self, shriveled behind a bag of loose skin, flabby muscles and brittle bones.

Why wouldn't I be worried about aging? I believed that if I were no longer playing in the sexual arena, or if I weren't a rich old person, I would be abandoned. I feared I'd be feeble, dependent and sexless, eating sticky spaghetti without sauce. Even young people worry about aging in a society that throws its old people out. No wonder some people spend more time worrying about being old than they do being old.

"The difference between worrying about being old and aging is that we can do something about worrying," Charlie said laughing. Then he added, "If you change your beliefs you can change."

After looking closely at my beliefs, I felt like I'd invented original sin . . . and I was ready for original thought.

I decided to imagine myself as a champion old person. I heard my inexhaustible voice booming from my still-strong body. I saw myself surrounded by beautiful old men leching after me, and I looked graceful, satisfied and tired. I imagined as many wrinkles on my soul as on my face, and as many friends to touch as there were to love.

Instead of imagining little, mean men with pitchforks waiting for me when I died, or envisioning white-winged angels on fluffy clouds, I began to see myself being born again on some distant star.

I had believed that we're born alone and we die alone, and that loneliness was a fact of life. Naturally I worried about being lonely. I knew nobody would speak to me if I divorced my husband.

"Why are most people I know lonely?" I asked Charlie.

"Because society has created a great gap between who we are and who we think we're supposed to be. People need to belong, to identify with our species. Hermits are just people with a sense of belonging with other hermits."

"What to do?" I asked.

"Loneliness, like most culturally-induced diseases, is curable with the ABC's of living."

I listened to Charlie as if my ears were new-found antennas to higher consciousness.

"Accept: What is . . . *is*. Belong: People need each other. Commit: Live the song you sing."

I watched the lights in Charlie's eyes twinkle like dancing stars when he added, "Life's a giant classroom, and every day and every lifetime brings us different lessons."

"You know so much Charlie, I'll bet you're glad you're not standing in my shoes."

"You're going to learn that there's a goddess in your shoes," Charlie said brightly.

"I'm afraid to ask, but what's a goddess?"

"A goddess is an ordinary woman when she's not afraid."

Late that night, I sat in front of my mirror and saw myself with kinder eyes. "Accept . . . Belong . . . Commit" soothed me. I accepted who I was even though who I was wasn't even close to who I wanted to be. I liked belonging with other people. I knew that if I really wanted to commit to living my life like a song, I'd have to start learning the score.

As I looked into my eyes, I began to see stars. Suddenly, instead of seeing creases, circles and scars, I saw stars! As I gazed into those stars, the fear of death and dying disappeared. I knew that if I really lived my life, I wouldn't be afraid to die.

ORANGE WATER TASTE

Location: *sex organs*

Sound: *VAM*

Color: *orange*

Element: *water*

Function: *sex*

Sense: *taste*

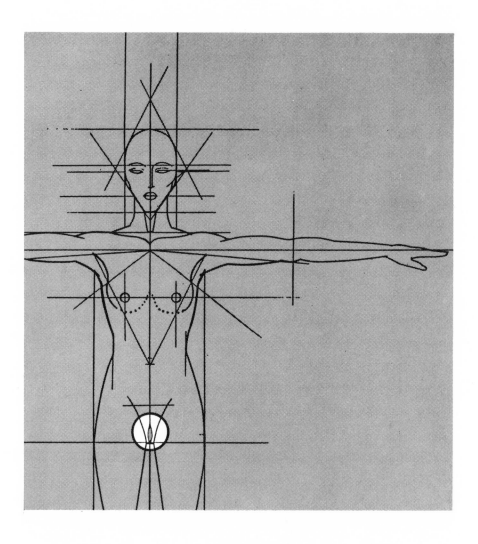

Issues

PHYSIOLOGICAL issues include disorders of the sex organs and spleen; urinary tract and reproductive system cysts, tumors and infections; low back pain; drying-out diseases such as arthritis and hardening of the arteries (everything dries up without intercourse); and loss of taste for food, sex and life. Balanced physical functioning brings easy absorption of nutrients.

EMOTIONAL/BEHAVIORAL issues deal with lack of sexual satisfaction and include sexual dysfunctions such as nymphomania, frigidity, impotence and premature ejaculation. Also included are problems with displaced sexual tension: masturbation, wet dreams, nightmares, lip biting; as well as excessive talking, lying, smoking, and excessive eating or drinking. Balanced emotional functioning brings sexual satisfaction.

SPIRITUAL issues concern separation of love and sex, inability to distinguish creativity from genital arousal, or general denial of sexual energy as such. Balanced spiritual functioning integrates the creative, healing power of sexuality with its transcendent qualities.

Questions

- How important is sex in my life?
- Am I perverted, weird, bad, good, frigid, over-sexed?
- Why do I feel guilty?
- What about masturbation?
- Can I control my desires?
- What's with my fantasies?
- How much pleasure is too much?
- Do I taste nice? Am I a sex object?
- Why am I not a sex object?
- What about commitment? Can monogamy work?

2

Sexuality

The Divinity of Sex

It was never God's intention
That this marvelous invention
  Human sexuality
Would give us all neuroses
Even some psychoses
That was never meant to be.
It was surely God's desire
That making love inspire
  Us to rise above
An endless search for pleasure
And use this sacred treasure
As a source of endless love.

S exuality is the perfume of the rose, the
plumage of the peacock, the gleam in the eye.
It's the essence of who we are. It's Freud's libido, DaVinci's art,
Mozart's music, and it was my nemesis.

It doesn't matter whether I blamed religion, my mother or Queen
Victoria, sex was shrouded in double messages, double standards and
double binds. Of course I felt guilty. I was programmed for guilt and
controlled with it. From the suck of my thumb at six months, to
playing doctor at six years, I was given guilt. "Bad little girl. That's
not nice. Don't touch. You'll go blind, hairy or mad." My adolescence
was treated like a contagious disease. How can people manage to
declare a natural biological function illegal? Masturbation is our first
play. If we don't learn to play with ourselves, how can we learn to play
with other people?

I used to fantasize about coming home from school feeling tired
and restless . . . and there was Mom, smiling at me from behind a
batch of fresh baked cookies saying, "You look so tense, sweetheart.
Why not go to your room and play with yourself before dinner?"

I tried repressing my sexual energy, but it was like trying to stuff
a tornado into a paper sack. I repressed it so much it popped up by
itself in my eating, drinking, smoking, lip biting, lying, shop lifting,
and dreams. When I wasn't thinking about sex, I was talking about it. I
saw sex in everything; a bee sucking nectar embarassed me as much

as a long loaf of French bread. I turned red just knowing I was naked under my clothes.

One sultry afternoon, a neighborhood boy stopped by uninvited. He caught me playing with myself and said I'd heard the call of the devil. I knew he was wrong, because "Idle hands are the devil's workshop," and mine had been busy all afternoon. Although I'd been taught that my sexual urges were sinful, I never bought it. I knew anything that felt this good, couldn't be bad.

Now, after a divorce, a nervous breakdown, and a year of celibacy, I made a list of 182 of my most pressing questions. They ranged from the ridiculous, "Is multiple orgasm possible after ninety?" to the sublime, "Is it possible to be sexy and holy, too?"

I concluded I was confused about sex. That's not surprising since I grew up believing that nice girls don't; they don't even like to. We weren't allowed to do it until we married, and then we had to do it whether we liked it or not. Humans always do it. When society said, "Don't do it," we did it anyway and got punished by mother. Now, society says, "Have at it," we do, and catch the wrath of Mother Nature.

During my marriage, sex had been high drama: simulated passion and award-winning fake orgasms. Suddenly, I was free to do it with anybody, and guilt contorted my body into one giant question mark. I was torn between wanting to give myself . . . and catching something.

I knew promiscuity is painful. That's not a moral judgement, it's a fact. Promiscuity prevents peace. Thanks to VD, herpes and AIDS, a one-night-stand could last forever. To avoid feeling guilty on my only one-night-stand, I convinced myself that this was going to be the most significant relationship of my life. Boy, was I surprised when I saw his picture in the paper! I hadn't even known his real name.

When I talked to Charlie about my confusion, he said, "Confusion happens when your mind doesn't want to hear what your heart is saying."

Suddenly, I realized the immorality of faking orgasms. By pretending to be enjoying a satisfactory sex life, I had been supporting goals, values, and a lifestyle I didn't respect. I didn't respect myself either. Now that I had less confusion, I had more guilt.

When I asked Charlie if it was possible to stop feeling guilty, he said, "You're in the *habit* of feeling guilty."

"Naturally," I said, "the whole society's waiting for me to screw up. It gives them something to do."

"Guilty people are easy to control," Charlie smiled. Then he said, "Feeling guilty is a bad habit you can exchange for a good habit, but you can't break a habit you don't know you have." I made a list of everything I did with regularity. I did everything regularly. There were so few things I did spontaneously, I couldn't remember what they were. My life was simply a succession of habits. I told the same stories, wore the same colors, ate the same foods, drove too fast, lied about my age, waited until the last minute to pay my taxes, bragged about everything, read in the toilet, drank coffee every day, criticized everyone, shopped at the same stores. It was depressing. Between my habits and beliefs, I was completely on automatic pilot. I figured that if I didn't replace unwanted habits with other habits, my activities would be so minimal, people might think I was dead.

Down my habit list I went, diligently replacing those I no longer liked. I stopped smoking, and began taking deep breaths instead. I stopped saving money and started spending it. I stopped taking Valium, and stayed up all night. Instead of standing in line like everybody else, I balanced on one leg. Instead of reading in the toilet, I wrote. I brushed my teeth, ate my meals and signed my name with my left hand, instead of my right. My checks bounced, I got three cavities, and I was almost arrested for running through a supermarket.

Worrying was a habit that worried me. "How did I get into the habit of worrying?" I worried. I tried to remember a time when I didn't worry. I couldn't. I always worried. I had heard, "You're a worrier," ever since I could bite my own nails. I knew it was a mental distraction that kept me from knowing what was really going on, and that it was never the big stuff like divorce or death, that would make me grey, but worrying about things that never happened that would kill me. But it wasn't until I began to worry about how I looked when I was worrying, that I committed to changing my habit.

Every time I began to worry about something, I would con- sciously say to myself, "TASE: Think About Something Else." *TASE* became a recipe for changing my worrying mind. *TASE, TASE, TASE* became my first mantra, and I would repeat it until I thought about something else. But changing had become a full-time job, and I was still feeling guilty.

Charlie was laughing, "Congratulations. You're a champion habit changer, but what is it you want?"

"The same thing the whole world wants: a lot of love, a few good laughs, and a little peace."

Charlie said, "You're too caught up in your habits to be loving, you take yourself too seriously to laugh whole-heartedly, and inner peace takes practice."

Confusion returned. My mind giving my heart a hard time.

Charlie smiled his "I love you" smile and said, "Why worry? You're a combination of your habits and beliefs. You're normal."

"Not any more," I said. "I resolve to erase my personal history and I hereby drop all my beliefs. As of this minute, I don't believe anything."

Driving home, I began to worry if I knew anything at all. I
questioned whether any of my beliefs were valid. At a red light, I saw
two women holding hands. I watched them and wondered if they did
it, and how. Then I visualized them doing it and instead of my old
beliefs, I began to wonder if homosexuality could be nature's way of
regulating the population of the planet without war. Perhaps if people
could get turned on to someone of the opposite sex, they could get
turned on to someone of the same sex, if they wanted to. I questioned
whether the reason I'd only been sexual with a man was because I
believed it was wrong to be sexual with a woman.

That week I let myself be seduced by a beautiful woman who
took me to her room and brought me to my senses. She loved me
uninhibitedly. She was so tender, she shattered my prejudices. I no
longer believed there could be more to a homosexual relationship than
sex, I knew it.

I saw how each of my habits supported a belief. For example, I
was in the habit of bleaching my hair blonde, because I believed
blondes had more fun.

I wondered how I had come to believe that women are not as
sexual as men, that my genitals were disgraceful, that once-a-week sex
was a lot, that multiple orgasms were a myth, that breath without
mouthwash caused abandonment, and that I needed a penis the way a
lifeguard needs ice skates.

As a kid I believed that sex was dangerous. Why wouldn't I? It
always got me in trouble. So I developed that habit of fantasizing
about it. It takes a good imagination to have a great fantasy, and my
fantasies beat the truth. Whether neurotic or erotic, fantasies kept me
sane.

When I was adolescent, I visualized my dad, tall and dignified,
standing at the door of my room saying, "I'm so proud you were
elected Sexiest Girl at school. I know you'll grow up and be a
wonderful woman and a great lay." Once I fantasized my grandmother
sitting at the edge of my bed, her grey hair glistening in the moonlight
saying, "I pray you use your remarkable sexual energy as a gateway to
God. It may be a back door, but I've hollered 'Oh God' a lot more
while coming with your grandaddy, than I ever did in church."

When Charlie said, "You're in the habit of feeling guilty," I
immediately made a guilt list. At the top of the list was, "I feel guilty
for lusting after a close friend's husband." I wanted absolution. I
believed if I confessed, I'd be healed.

"Hello Doris? This is Me. I'm calling to apologize for seducing
your husband . . . No. Oh no! It was twenty years ago and nothing
really happened. I just hadn't learned to channel my sexual energy."

Doris didn't remember my name. How could she? I'd changed it
three times since she knew me. I couldn't calm her down before she

hung up, and I spent a week . . . feeling guilty.

"Can I change?" I lamented to Charlie.

"Those who don't want to change, will stay the same."

"But I do want to change," I said emphatically.

"Those who want to change, won't stay the same."

That night, after a hot bath, I took the phone off the hook and went to bed early. I closed my eyes and visualized a man walking beside me on a country path. He was short (I'd always believed that only tall men had nice penises). He was bald (I'd believed only hairy men were handsome). He was thin (I had thought only gorilla types were virile). He smiled at me. His face was warm and loving and he invited me into his outstretched arms. He wasn't overtly sexual, just nurturing. He held me and I began to cry (I believed men wouldn't tolerate a woman's tears). Soft, sweet tears of relief came at finally feeling safe and understood.

He had me sit next to him under a tree (I'd believed people got grass stains and bug bites from sitting on the ground). This was paradise. We talked to each other (I'd believed men only talked to women about what they wanted for dinner). The birds sang for us, the sun shined for us, and we danced and played and swayed with the rhythm of the universe. He held me close and told me he wanted me to do whatever I wanted, only what would make me happy and joyous. I reached out and touched his face tentatively, then I fell into his soulful eyes.

Without hesitating I told him I wanted to make love with him (I'd believed that only the man could initiate a sexual encounter). He smiled knowingly and reassuringly, and, keeping his eyes intensely focused on mine, began slowly stroking my naked face (I believed women without makeup were either lazy or gay).

He told me with his eyes and his hands, as well as his words, that I was a goddess, and he wanted to make worship on me. We lay on the ground together and he began to caress my toes with a tenderness I'd never known. He sweetly stroked the hair under my arms (I'd believed underarm hair was a mistake of nature). His touch was as gentle as the dew drops on a lily. He kissed my eye lids with little licks of his tongue. He nibbled at my finger tips. He scratched my head affectionately. He sucked the lobe of my ear until I felt an intense desire to love and be loved. He stroked my fingers as if they were a magical instrument of God, sent to resonate heavenly sound on Earth.

I responded with sighs, sneezes and heavy coughing . . . but I did wake up knowing I would find my mate.

The next morning, I telephoned the man I had a date with that evening and cancelled, knowing I was changing . . . and fast.

Back at the ashram, I was changing my body. I was doing an exercise called Sat Kriya. I was sitting on my heels, my arms

straight up in the air, my palms pressed together. You're supposed to breathe and pump the navel point in and out while simultaneously pulling up on the muscles of the anus and genitals. This was an exercise I'd never managed to do for the full seven minutes. I always managed to die before the time was up. It demanded perseverence, practice and stamina. An altered state of consciousness and a good night's sleep would have helped.

Believing I couldn't make it through the exercise anyway, I began to cheat. I was just holding my arms up relatively close to my ears, hoping to make it look good. Just then the teacher said, "Don't cheat yourself." His words penetrated my otherwise preoccupied brain.

I felt as though I'd betrayed my country, sold my children into slavery, and offered my dog for vivesection. I knew the meaning of shame.

Suddenly I knew the difference between guilt and shame. It wasn't guilt I felt for holding my two-year-old's hands on those hot scrambled eggs in that restaurant when she wouldn't stop crying . . . it was shame. Guilt came from breaking the laws imposed by society; shame came from violating my inner code of conduct. To stop feeling guilty, I needed to be forgiven. . . . To stop feeling shame, I had to forgive myself.

"Ten seconds," the teacher said. I pumped my belly, pulled my muscles and heard, "The moment you accept yourself exactly as you are, you will be transformed." I pumped and pulled for all I was worth . . . and I made it. Slowly, my arms floated down, like feathers. I was filled with emptiness, a peaceful, quiet calm. Then waves of pleasure flooded me. I sat absolutely still, listening to my body. I trusted it. My body was the one consistent, reliable source of truth I could count on. The pain of guilt was gone, and in its place was pleasure. I had always heard that guilt hurts, that pain prevents pleasure. But until I let the guilt go and experienced the disappearance of that pain, I had no idea how much pleasure I could have.

"Charlie," I said, practically bursting with joy, "you are looking at a guilt-free woman who knows what she wants! I want more pleasure. I want to laugh and dance and make love to abandon. Is that hedonistic?"

"It's intelligent." He smiled wide.

"It hasn't been easy being sexy, Charlie, but even sexy people need love."

"And even loving people need sex," Charlie laughed.

"I want both. I want to turn my sex drive into a magic carpet, but I can't do it alone. Medicinal sex is good medicine, no matter what my mother says, but I want more than a succession of loving lays. I want a succession of loving lays with a lover who wants the ecstasy two people can experience when they're willing to commit themselves to each other. I want someone with sensitive hands, an open mind, and a willing heart; a partner who wants to discover the limitless healing potential that can come from the conscious weaving of a tapestry of sacred sex. . . . That's it! . . . Charlie, I want a man who doesn't screw around!"

"Anyone enjoying a blissful, satisfying, erotic sex life is a lot less likely to go for a roll in the hay," Charlie mused. "But remember, good sex is great, and great sex takes practice."

"Sign me up, Charlie. I don't want to be just guilt-free, I want to be sexy and holy, too."

Convinced that even Joan of Arc liked having orgasms, and believing that my new guilt-free state would enable me to go from mundane to sacred sex, I had an attack of euphoria. I decided to share my joy with my mother. In retrospect, it's easy to see I had simply lost my mind.

I wanted to reassure her that no matter what she had done to cause me guilt, it didn't matter. I wanted to forgive and forget, to be loving. After all, I was a guilt-free woman now, and now was all we had. Now, I would stay meditative and calm.

Driving to her house, I began thinking about why I used to feel sooo guilty for letting Michael Bradshaw put his fingers inside my panties . . . now I realized it was because she'd carved "whore" into the cover of my leather-bound high school year book, when she found out. I remembered how guilty I'd felt for hating her for breaking up my relationship with the only boy I ever loved . . . now I remembered that she'd told his mother I was a very sick girl with a dangerously weak heart. I remembered feeling ashamed for not breast-feeding my babies . . . now I realized how she'd accused me of deliberately trying to embarrass her to death with such a barbaric custom. I thought about how guilty I felt for divorcing my rich husband . . . now I realized that she'd convinced me my divorce had caused her heart attack.

I wasn't very calm or meditative by the time I remembered how guilty I used to feel for smoking marijuana and telling my children it was tobacco from another planet . . . because she'd threatened to have me arrested if I smoked it.

I breathed deep at every traffic light, struggling to keep my composure. When I reached her house, she opened the door and I screamed, "I'm a guilt-free woman and I'll fuck anybody I please!"

It was three months before she'd talk to me, and that's only because I begged her to. . . . I was feeling sooooo guilty.

YELLOW FIRE SIGHT

Location :	*solar plexus*
Sound :	*RAM*
Color :	*yellow*
Element :	*fire*
Function :	*power*
Sense :	*sight*

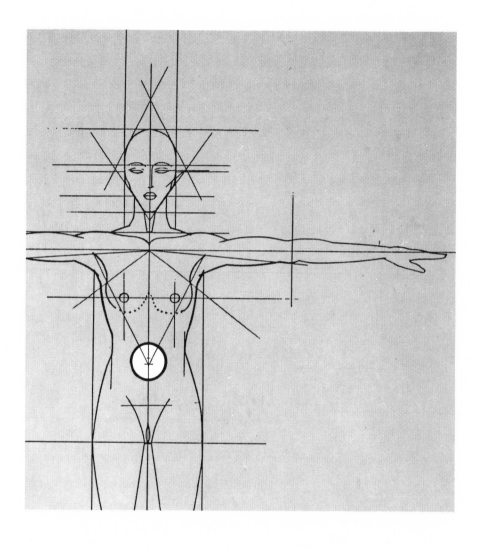

Issues

PHYSIOLOGICAL issues include disorders of the solar plexus and belly, digestive disorders such as stomach ulcers, and eating disorders such as anorexia and bulimia. Also included are problems with vision. Balanced physical functioning brings good digestion.

EMOTIONAL/BEHAVIORAL issues deal with lack of power which results in problems with anger, longing, violence, stubbornness, rage, competition, bullish aggression, driving ambition, temper tantrums, over-emotionality, passive-aggression, manipulation, a need to be right. Balanced emotional functioning brings a sense of humor and the spirit of play.

SPIRITUAL issues concern conflict between "My will be done," and "Thy will be done." Balanced functioning aligns individual will with Divine Will. Imbalance focuses on power-over, and balance becomes power-to.

Questions

- Why am I so angry?
- Who do I blame?
- How can I be myself?
- How can I get weaned?
- How can I get independent?
- When is it MY time?
- Why must I control everything and everyone?
- Why am I so competitive?
- What am I longing for?
- Why do I either starve or stuff myself?

3

Will Power

Become Whoever You Are

In the game of life, I was a pawn
Sacrificed every sunset and dawn
> *The game had been played*
> *By parents who prayed*
For a son, a dog and a lawn.
It was hard to survive that difficult scene
Not because my parents were mean
> *They had wanted a Knight*
> *And I took delight*
In becoming a radiant Queen.

O ne good scream is worth a thousand words. Charlie had said that if I wanted inner peace, I would have to make peace with my parents. It would have been easier to negotiate a treaty between the United States and Russia, guaranteeing immediate disarmament and eternal peace, love and brotherhood.

I sometimes fantasized meetings between the heads of state of the USSR and the USA. They would be sitting close to each other wearing comfortable cotton leisure suits. Several top brass officers would be standing around looking relaxed and smiling.

The president of the USA reaches over and takes the Russian leader's hand and says warmly, "Let's drop all our defenses. There's no need to fight anymore. What do you say? Want to bury the hatchet and forgive each other our mistakes?"

The Russian chairman smiles wide and says, "Let's do it, Mr. President. Let's cooperate with each other so we can enjoy a little peace. I'll never again mention all the wrongs you've done us, like that bomb you dropped on Tivoli. I happened to have had a few relatives there at the time, or I wouldn't even make a fuss. But I'm willing to forgive and forget."

"So am I," the president says. "We don't have to hold grudges. I won't even remind you of the havoc you caused when you dropped that stupid nuclear shit all over our East Coast. Let's forget it, all right?"

The heads of state needed a miracle to pull it off. So did my parents and I.

My parents had written a script for my life's drama before I was born. The further I got from the character I was supposed to play, the more angry, worried and confused they got. The more difficult they made it for me to individuate, the angrier I became. Since most of this process was happening without any of us knowing it, it was practically impossible to negotiate for anything more than a few reasonably peaceful minutes every now and then.

Fresh anger is healthy. People's faces flush with a rosy glow, their eyes get bright, they become animated and lively. My anger was ancient and so stale it was making me sick. It was like carrying around a huge sack of garbage on my back, and I was looking for some place to dump it. No wonder I slumped.

Anger and blame go together like trees and a forest, and it's difficult to perceive something that's staring you in the face.

I was not only angry, I blamed my parents for everything: the war in the Middle East, my flunking algebra, even my divorce (because if it hadn't been for them, I wouldn't have gotten married in the first place). "If it weren't for you" was our favorite game. We all played. Blaming was easy. It was a habit, and it made me feel so innocent.

I knew that dependency fosters anger and blame, and that sooner or later, we resent those on whom we depend. I had no trouble recognizing that I was dependent on my parents for their approval. What I didn't understand was why! I disapproved of almost everything they did and it didn't seem to bother them.

In graduate school, I was learning sophisticated techniques for marriage and family counseling. In the hospital, I was the psychology intern people turned to in their time of trouble and need. In my home, I was the modern single mother, parenting in absentia. With my parents, I was having seizures. My daughters would counsel me, "Relax, Mom, it's hopeless."

My teachers said that we all had to accept responsibility for ourselves; that we were not victims, but agents of our own destiny; our first responsibility was to ourselves. It sounded great, I just couldn't convince my mother. She believed I should take care of her and put my own life on hold. After all, why else did people have children? They were expensive in the beginning, but they were supposed to pay off in the end. I didn't know who I was, so how could I know to whom and to what I was responsible!

I knew it was difficult for my parents to see me as an adult . . . because "they knew me when." My parents believed I'd taken a short detour and that I would remarry, return to the sanctuary of the suburbs, and never embarrass them again. I believed if I didn't get weaned, I'd never know myself and it would be impossible for us to ever be close and loving.

Becoming my Self required will power. Without it, I was like a
little lamb with dark glasses: following blindly. I compromised and
married a man I not only loved, but who I knew they would approve
of.

The criticism I was force-fed for my sexuality was baby food
compared to what I got for asserting my will. "You're going to India to
do *what?* Are you stupid or crazy? You ought to be ashamed of
yourself, wearing some idiot's picture around your neck like that." Or
I would hear, "Don't tell me you're leaving your children and the most
wonderful man in the world, home alone . . . again."

The fact that my children were already grown and almost as old
as I was, and that I'd separated from my husband, made no difference
at all.

I knew my parents had programmed me and that their tapes were
still playing in my head. I had to be re-programmed. I needed to be re-
parented and I needed new messages and new role models to do it. I
would fantasize some gorgeous goddess or movie star as my mother,
some equally magnificent man as my father, and I'd take their
messages personally.

I would pick a fear or phobia, like my anxiety about diving from a
high dive at a swimming pool. Then I would remember a scene from
my childhood when that fear began. I'd lie down and visualize the
scene: I was standing on the high diving board. I was six or seven,
skinny, rambunctious, determined. Just as I was ready to dive, my
mother screamed, "Don't jump! Don't jump! For God's sake somebody stop her. My child's about to kill herself." That was the moment
I decided to be afraid to dive!

Then, I would lie still, breathe deep, and imagine the scene again.
This time my mother was a mermaid. She looked at me about to dive
and yelled, "That's a girl. You can do it. Go on, you're a great diver."
And I would see myself diving fearlessly.

It wasn't as hard to learn new tricks as it was to unlearn the old
ones. I had become counter-phobic. If my parents were afraid of
something, I either embraced it or brought it home for dinner. My
mother was afraid of animals; my house was a zoo. She was anti-sex; I
planned to become a high priestess of spiritual love-making. My
parents were afraid of planes; I sky-dived. They were big on organized
religion; the only church I would consider was United Orgasm.

I had not shared esoteric or spiritual experiences with my parents
since I was eleven and tried to explain that I had an orgasm and saw
God. They reacted to anything they didn't understand with fear and
denial.

When I told them I was accompanied by an eagle and a lion, they
bought mental health insurance.

"You're not starting to see people in color again, are you?" Or I
heard, "I'm certain there's a logical explanation for how you knew
that, dear."

It wasn't easy being parented, and parenting wasn't any easier. When my daughters complained about me, I reassured them it was never too late to get re-parented. With enough therapy, a few workshops, and a lobotomy, they'd have no trouble forgetting what I'd taught them.

When I was staff psychologist in an alcoholism rehabilitation hospital, my daughter announced that she was going to bartender's school. "Fine," I growled, "just change your name and when you pass me on the street, act like you don't know me."

"What's so wrong with alcohol?" she asked, lighting her cigarette: "We all need to alter our consciousness, don't we?"

"Sure," I said, pretending not to notice the smoke, "but the trick is to find healthy, fun ways of doing it."

"Frankly, Mom, if I lived the lifestyle of most of the alcoholics I know, I wouldn't get sober either. Alcoholics are too sensitive and intelligent to withstand the pressure of the reality they're surrounded with."

As I watched her deeply inhale her cigarette smoke I said, "But nicotine's as dangerous as alcohol. Society seduces us into using both of them, neglects to tell us how addictive they are, makes us feel guilty about our addictions, then charges us a fortune to help us withdraw."

"So how can people alter their consciousness?" She seemed to be listening.

"What about jogging, dancing, yoga, swimming, meditation?" I deliberately left out marijuana.

"Doctors claim aerobic dancing is as dangerous as meditation, runners risk arthritis, biting dogs and death by auto . . . and marijuana's illegal because it's one of the greatest sources of revenue for the government, besides . . . if the military smokes, they won't fight."

The conversation taught me two things. First, expecting my daughter to agree with me was like believing I would suddenly agree with my parents. Second, expecting an alcoholic to return to the same boring or purposeless life-style and stay sober was like promising celibacy to a nymphomaniac as a reward for not screwing around.

One Monday morning, while desperately trying to conceal a terrible hangover, I asked a patient patronizingly, "Did you drink while you were out on pass this weekend?"

"Did you?" the patient asked back. "You rehab racketeers treat us patients as if we were different from you."

I wondered if he knew I had a hangover.

Our rehab program had been conceived by a dedicated psychiatrist with enthusiasm and heart. He knew the importance of touch and the danger of hierarchy. He was driven out and replaced by a staff sovereign, a mercenary masquerading as a doctor.

I looked around at the rest of the staff. We were all normal healthy neurotics doing the best we could. There was one heavy drinking anorexic, a Rajneeshi, one borderline, an obsessive-compulsive, a promiscuous flake, one ego-maniac, and a few well-intentioned chronic-undifferentiated assholes. We believed we had all the answers. It was clear that what we all had, patients and staff alike, were the same: "thou shalts," "thou shalt nots," and "thou-better-not-even-think-about-its." We were all struggling to find meaning and purpose in our lives. The only difference between patients and staff was who carried the keys to the doctor's lounge.

"What is alcoholism?" I asked Charlie after I'd spent three years on staff at the hospital.

"It's Staying Sickness," he said. "We either have Original Sickness, like being born with one foot missing; or Wandering Sickness, which comes from catching something that's wandering around (like a virus); or we have Staying Sickness which comes from improper reaction to power objects."

It was as if somebody moved the trees out of the way so I could see the forest. "Could a power object be a boss, or a parent, or a spouse, or a doctor, of . . .?"

"Naturally," Charlie smiled. "Alcoholism, like all psychosomatic diseases, comes as a result of the way we react to power."

It was clear how my improper reaction to my power objects (my parents) was causing me to lose sight of any real purpose in life. I was so busy doing the opposite of what they wanted, I had no time to do what I wanted. I didn't even know what it was I wanted.

"Why am I so defended?" I asked my Self.

"Because," I realized, "I need to protect my personal power, that's why."

I assumed that I had inherited my defensiveness along with my crooked toe. The instant I became curious, I dropped my defenses. The less defensive I became, the more curious I got. Now I was starting to see that if my purpose in life was to grab for more, bigger, better things, I would stay defensive . . . and greedy.

Life is a search for personal power. We all need it and we all grab for it. I had used sex, money, drugs, my role and my position to grab at it. Using sex to gain power is like screwing a slot machine . . . it's cold as steel and we rarely hit the jackpot.

I tried using sex appeal with my father once when I was young, but he leaped out of his chair so fast, I fell on the floor. I had experimented with cocaine to give me a sense of power. If things go better with coke, it's purely temporary. I paid for fifteen minutes of feeling like Superwoman, with days of depression, irritability, bloody nostrils, insomnia, guilt and an empty bank account. I found that any purpose without heart is a pseudo-purpose . . . it's a power trip.

I had developed considerable power through my ability to bio-energetically analyze people's faces and bodies. I knew, just by looking, whether people had siblings, if they had a harder time with their mother or father, whether or not they'd been breast fed, if they were or weren't orgasmic, etc. With bioenergetic analysis, I could be all-powerful, all-knowing, and feel nothing. But therapy without heart is like sex without love . . . it may help but it can't heal.

I integrated the heartfelt spiritual systems of kundalini yoga and shamanism with bioenergetic therapy, creating "tri-energetic" exercises that involved the spirit as well as the body and mind.

Then the new staff sovereign told me that I would no longer be allowed to hug my patients. I knew that I couldn't be therapeutic with someone I wasn't free to hug.

I marched into the next staff meeting and announced that we were causing our patients to have improper reactions to power objects because we played "me-doctor . . . you-patient" games. I fearlessly recommended a few extra hugs a day to break down the barriers between patients and staff.

The new chief, who was charging a hundred dollars for a ten-minute chat with patients, had difficulty letting go of a need for power and control, and fired me.

I worked out my frustrations at the ashram. We were doing a very difficult kundalini yoga exercise called Stretch Pose. I was lying on my back; my arms, legs and head raised six inches from the floor. I was breathing rapidly through my nose, pumping my navel center with each breath. The technique is called, appropriately, Breath of Fire. We were to hold the position for three minutes, which was two-and-a-half minutes longer than I could manage.

I began to complain, "I have weak legs . . . I have gas . . . I've had three babies . . . I can't do this shit."

Then I heard, "Tolerate, change or be grateful."

Instead of giving up, I consciously changed the intolerable position by using different muscles. Instead of straining as I was in the habit of doing, I relaxed into the position. All of a sudden, I don't know why, I stretched my hands out as far as I could and let my thumbs touch the tops of my legs. It was as if I had stuck them into a socket and gotten all the juice I needed. My thumbs felt like electrified hooks holding my legs up for me.

Then it happened. I began to see pictures, clear images of my parents as young children. I saw my mother first. She was about six years old, lonely and frightened. She was clutching a small rag doll. Someone I didn't know, a tall blond man, was terrorizing her. He had a sadistic look on his face. I felt like protecting her. I wanted to help her and comfort her and tell her I understood.

Then I saw my father. He was a small boy, around eight or nine, and he was lost in a wood. He was frantic, desperately trying to find his way out. He tried to call out, but he began to sob pathetically. I ached to rescue him, to tell him he was safe and that I loved him.

The next thing I knew, the teacher was saying, "Relax."

I collapsed onto the floor. I didn't understand what I had seen, nor did I know whether those scenes had actually happened to my parents. What I did realize, without doubt, was that I was the child of lonely, frightened children who were doing the best they could.

I left the ashram and drove directly to my parents' house. This time I wasn't out of my mind, I was into my heart. "Tolerate, change or be grateful" circled around my head until it made a wrinkle in my brain. I knew I couldn't tolerate some of my parents ways, their teachings, their life-style, their need to control me. I definitely could not change them. I could either complain . . . or be grateful. I had an attack of gratitude. I knew that my parents were martyrs and messengers. In the ultimate wisdom of the universe, they had taught me how *not* to be.

I stopped for a traffic light and imagined a pamphlet entitled *Parenting*. "There are no perfect parents, and that's perfect. . . . Good enough parenting is great." I drove to the nearest parking lot, stopped the engine and made notes. "Parents control with guilt." I sighed, grateful I wasn't buying any. "Parents control with money." Luckily, mine didn't have any. "Good parents strive to become unnecessary." Mine had made it. "All parents cause pain and trouble. They either hang on or tear loose. They either teach too much or not enough, touch too much or not enough, love too much or not enough. They provide what they can, and that's never enough. They give and take, forgive and make mistakes, but they always do the best they can."

I drove on towards my parents' house. "How does anyone ever know if she's been a successful parent?" I wondered, thinking how many people were paying for my counsel and my kids didn't return my phone calls. Suddenly, I realized that I was doing the best I could, and the question disappeared.

When my mother opened the door, I took her in my arms for the first time in years and said, "I love you."

STOP doing things because they are meaningful to others. If I want to do them do so because they are meaningful to me!!

GREEN AIR TOUCH

Location:	*heart*
Sound:	*YAM*
Color:	*green*
Element:	*air*
Function :	*love*
Sense:	*touch*

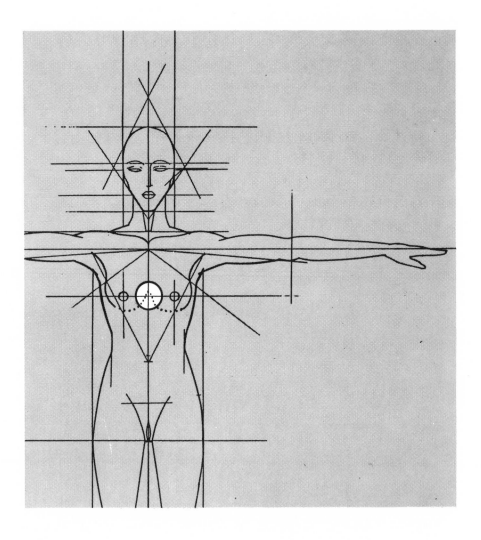

Issues

PHYSIOLOGICAL issues include disorders of the heart, lungs and thymus gland: heart and lung disease, chest pain, shortness of breath, circulation problems, cold hands and feet, immune system deficiency, etc. Balanced physical functioning brings disease resistance.

EMOTIONAL/BEHAVIORAL issues deal with lack of love: melancholy, fear of touch, problems with intimacy, confusion, lack of empathy. Balanced emotional functioning brings joy, laughter, compassion, and love.

SPIRITUAL issues concern transforming the first three chakras with love, and knowing when to open the floodgates of compassion and when to close the heart for self-preservation.

Questions

- Will anybody love me?
- Am I capable of loving someone totally?
- Is it love or infatuation?
- What's the difference between love and being-in-love?
- Is God Love?
- Is Compassion Love?
- What is a true friend?
- Am I anyone's best friend?
- Do I love my environment?
- Does love start with me?
- Do I have to love myself to love someone else?
- Do I have to love myself to have someone love me?

4

Love

Amazing Me

Amazing me I've finally found
There's nobody left to blame.
I'm me! I'm free!
And now I know I'll never be the same.

(sung to the tune of *Amazing Grace*)

L ife goes better with love.
     My heart was brimming full of compassion
and understanding. I believed I had transcended my personal problems and awakened to a cosmic consciousness that would change my
life . . . until my mother said, "You've been smoking marijuana,
haven't you?"

I had been struggling to gain freedom *from* . . . from oppression,
from the burden of culture; freedom from old beliefs and habits. Now,
with my heart open, I wanted freedom *to* . . . to do what I wanted. I
kissed my mother good-by before we hit each other, and left.

Charlie was waiting at home. "We have to feel safe to be loving,"
he offered.

I was as confused about love as I was about sex. They were both
confounded and defiled. I had been taught that on the one hand, love
was naive, foolish or unattainable. On the other hand, it was supposed
to be the ultimate purpose of life. I had always heard how much I was
loved, but somehow I never felt it. Non-verbal messages are so much
stronger than words that if someone says, "Of course I love you,"
through clenched teeth and glaring eyes, we get the message. Hearing
"I love you" and feeling loved are as different as being served a menu
and getting something to eat.

I had trouble differentiating between love and infatuation. As a
teenager, I sometimes found myself consumed with desire. Mostly, the
object of my infatuation was anybody who liked me. I was more
attracted to mathematical whiz-kid types, with little shoulders and big
glasses, but anybody who spoke nicely to me would do. I would get
that crazy, overwhelming feeling that consumed my every waking

moment, and a few sleepless nights. I would wait in anguish for phone calls I knew weren't coming. I would scheme, manipulate, and pray for the attention of the usually unsuspecting hero. Infatuation came as a distraction from the feelings of longing to be loved at home.

Once I fell in love with a boy who was two feet shorter than I was. I used to pray he would grow two feet overnight because no girl wants a boyfriend who comes up to her breast. I also prayed that I'd stop growing, because nobody wants a girlfriend eight feet tall.

I was convinced that love was something I had to earn. I always thought I had to do something to be loved. I could not remember ever being loved for simply being me. I had heard that love starts within. I couldn't even get away with liking myself. Once in school I thought it was cool to say I liked myself. That cured me. I was labeled Miss Conceited and tortured with, "There goes Stuck-up. She likes herself."

Besides, why should I love myself? I hadn't won Best Actress or Most Popular Girl or any merit badges in school. I lied, cheated, stole money from my aunt's purse, played with myself, and let Milton Down feel me up. How could I love myself?

I would rather have been loved than anything. Heart hunger hurts. I needed some soul food to end that hunger.

One day while driving through traffic, I turned on the tape player. I heard, "You are holy and perfect, exactly as you are. Stop trying to please everyone. You are entitled to unconditional love." I swerved my car, barely missing a bus, and pulled over to hear what I was listening to. A friend had put the tape in my car, intending to give me a little uplifting spiritual message. The voice was Bhagwan Rajneesh, who at the time was still seducing disciples in India. I listened carefully, letting his words and his voice come into my heart. I opened like a lotus in a steam room. Trying to avoid any rash decisions (I knew I looked awful in orange), I drove home and dyed all my clothes. I went to India to discover unconditional love. What I experienced was unrelenting diarrhea.

What was a Ph.D. doing on a squat toilet, desperately trying to dodge a dive-bombing kamikaze mosquito out for blood? Why was I subjected to the embarrassment of squatting right next to the only man at the ashram who interested me, who was having his own problems with Rama Krishna's Revenge? Why would a normal woman leave a safe and cozy kitchen for one that offered a smorgasbord of amoebic dysentery, hepatitis and worms? Why did I risk rides in rickshaws, driven by little brown stunt men who delighted in speeding up as soon as they knew I was terrified? Why did I leave my great bed, air-conditioning and privacy for a grass mat in a sweltering room I shared with a menagerie of bugs, critters and one fat rat?

I needed to belong!

There were so many people, just like me, who had never felt a sense of connectedness, that feeling of being part of a group in which we all shared a noble intention, a common goal and a lovable leader. I'd never been exposed to a group, or belonged to a group, who hugged each other for no reason at all. Every woman needs a sister, so does every man. I found myself surrounded by brothers and sisters, and for all the talk of free sex in Poona, I found it less promiscuous than the suburban breeding grounds I'd left behind. Even sexy people need friends.

We were given new names, new identities, new roles. My name was Satya, the truth, and since I always rearranged reality, I liked being identified with the truth for a change. It was a rebirth, a second chance. In India, with Rajneesh, I projected the highest human qualities onto each orange blossom, and so my new family was a bouquet of wisdom, truth, purity, love, compassion, light and grace. I didn't care if there were any blooming idiots under the robes. I belonged.

I had been studying hypnosis with some of the best psychologists in the USA. Now I was experiencing a master hypnotist who could mesmerize ten thousand people with the slur of his "s." Besides, he was cute. It wasn't until he began to take himself seriously that I began to doubt. I was in love with the teachings, not the teacher.

I had been searching for a role model. Rajneesh was it. He was graceful, articulate and loved by a hundred thousand people. Talk about social security.

The problem with gurus is not when they believe they're God . . . it's when they believe they're God and nobody else is that they irritate a lot of people. I found myself turned off to the need to prostrate myself before his Godly Assholiness . . . and still it took two years of wearing his picture around my neck, a wardrobe of nothing but orange, and the threat of being disowned by my children, to quit.

I returned home from India knowing that people who believe you can only get close to God if you recite mantras in golden temples, may never get to meet a holy person who drinks two beers at the local pub every night. I also knew I was still confused about unconditional love.

"A guru is someone who says what you agree with," Charlie said. "Guru stands for 'Gee, you are you!' "

I'd experienced amazing things in India but I hadn't realized that the magic came from the group, not the leader. I knew that one-on-one office therapy was limited to the energy generated by two people. If I was having an off day, and my client wasn't exactly on either, the session was like trying to start a fire with wet wood.

One afternoon, after friends had given me a T-shirt with removable letters, in case I decided to change my name again, I came home feeling defended, worried and confused. I sat down and began doing a

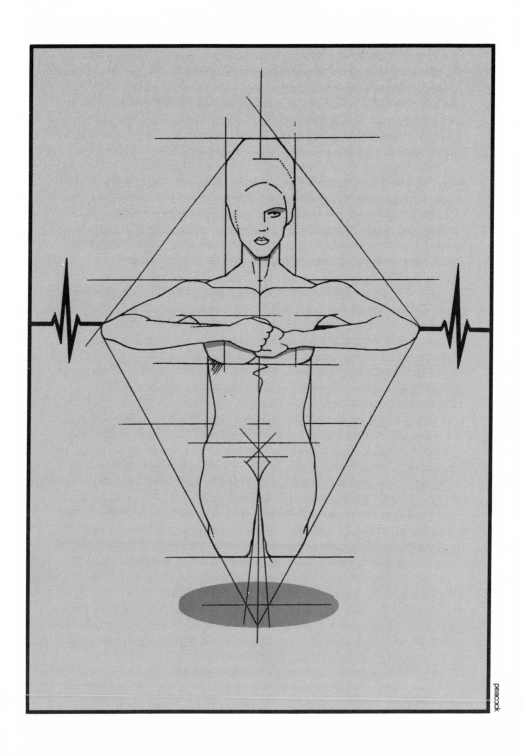

meditation to make my worries look small. It was supposed to be done for eleven minutes, but I usually did it for three with good results. I was sitting comfortably cross-legged, just getting into it, when suddenly I sneezed, my eyes opened, and I found myself staring into the brilliant brown eyes of Shiloh, my dog. A soft, sweet expression was covering her face, and her mouth was fixed in a silly, spectacular grin. She had been silently sitting beside me, looking satisfied. She wasn't expecting me to stop what I was doing, to change my posture, my hair color, or the way I drove my car. She wasn't complaining, criticizing or begging for something. She was just sitting there, smiling . . . and loving me. I reached over and touched her warm, furry little head. She closed her eyes, jutted out her long regal nose and pushed it into my hand, making herself clearly understood. "I love you," she said, with her whole canine being. I could feel her love for me . . . strong, absolute, and unconditional. My heart melted. I loved her whether she shit on the floor, got fur on the furniture, or threw up on my tax return. I loved her unconditionally. Love was, clearly, energy. It wasn't necessarily emotional. I wasn't in love with my dog. I loved her. It was an energy that seemed as natural as breathing.

I wasn't feeling defended, worried or confused anymore. I was curious, accepting and grateful. The intensity of that moment of unconditional acceptance opened the door to a whole new world. No statistic could measure the magnitude of an open heart.

Shiloh and I lay upon our yoga mat, breathing slowly. I wondered how it happened that for all the years we were together, I was never able to love her this deeply. I closed my eyes and remembered a time when I'd loved a puppy. Each day, I literally ran home to play and be with him. I loved that little dog so much. One day, before he'd outgrown chewing up staircases, eating my father's underwear, and shitting on every strategic spot in the house, my parents gave him away. I came home from school to an empty house . . . my dog was gone! My heart closed. The fear of losing a love like that again had kept me from loving Shiloh with all my heart. Only now and then, I would let in small homeopathic doses to keep myself nourished . . . enough to survive, but not to thrive.

Then I remembered something Charlie had said, "Fear and love are like oil and water . . . often in the same container, but they don't mix well."

I thought back to my school years. I'd believed that teachers, like Santa Claus, knew everything. They had supervision and zoomed-in on what I was doing in my home. They knew what I ate, how I slept, and who I talked to. It had been hard to love my teachers because mostly they relied on fear to keep the balance in the classroom. They had to . . . it was thirty-five against one.

Once in a great while, a good teacher came along, one who loved to teach. She usually only lasted a season or two before some Prince Charming came and swept her away, saving her from the system.

Only once a great teacher appeared, one who inspired the students to love learning. I remembered Mr. Ferris with absolute clarity. I was in third grade. He was tall, lanky, with sea-green eyes and a sweet smile. I stood at his desk after school one day and told him I wanted to marry him. I wanted to be his slave, to follow him around everywhere and devote myself to taking care of his every need . . . . forever.

I offered myself in an innocent seduction that Mr. Ferris handled with such tenderness and compassion, that it was a great teaching in itself. I loved him even more after that. He made learning ecstasy. He motivated me to be curious, to wake up, and to enjoy daydreaming. He was fired before the end of the term. I was convinced it was my fault. It was years later that I learned Mr. Ferris had been fired because he was gay.

Love and fear don't mix well, so how could I love people when half the human race scared me to death, and the other half terrified me! Of course I was fearful of men. They had the power to reduce me to a second-class citizen with one paycheck. Men could put me out to pasture with a three-inch drop in my tits. Why shouldn't I fear women? They were the enemy and armed to the teeth. How could I feel love with my family when I was either blaming them, or defending myself? I found it impossible to feel love at cocktail parties with people I hardly knew, seldom spoke to, and never touched.

Shiloh stretched languidly just then, and her little warm paws were gracefully poised like a soft-sculptured stuffed animal. I realized I'd never felt as close to God in any organized religious ceremony as I did looking into her eyes. At organized religious functions I was too afraid of wearing the wrong hat or shoes or color to feel comfortable. I had believed I had to like religion to love God. I hated religion. It was big business: stern and solemn, with no merriment or joy.

I stretched, too, and remembered the ABCs Charlie had taught me. Only now they were clearer somehow. Acceptance was easy with Shiloh. Belonging was natural: my dog and I belonged with each other. Commitment became obvious. I always had trouble trusting myself. Commitments were vague promises that, like most laws, were meant to be broken. Now, looking into the eyes of this trusting soul, I knew love meant trust, and she trusted me completely. I certainly trusted her. I wanted to make a commitment to her and said, "I'll never again buy that cheap dog food you can't stand." Shiloh's ears jutted forward, and she sat straight up. "And, I'll never abandon you in your old age," I said, crying.

I got up and wrote down a commitment to myself, "I commit to being more compassionate and forgiving . . . to myself and everyone around me." I turned the commitment into an affirmation, "I am compassionate and forgiving."

Each day, driving through traffic, standing in long lines on one leg, listening to my mother's complaints on the phone, working with the pains of my clients, I repeated the affirmation, "I am compassionate and forgiving."

When my daughter told me she had borrowed and burned my new gown, I said, "I'm compassionate and forgiving." When the hairdresser fried my hair, leaving me looking like my fingers were stuck in an electric socket, I silently said, "I am compassionate and forgiving." When the laundry lost my clothes, I told the woman, "I'm compassionate and forgiving." I got pretty good at it. I'd believed practice makes possible, now I knew it.

I understood the sufferings of my parents, and I forgave them for trying to mold me into someone they believed I should be. I forgave my husbands with whom I didn't belong, knowing we had done the best we could. I felt love and compassion for my surgeon ex-husband, knowing that even rich, sexy surgeons need love.

I knew a balanced life embraces the joys and sorrows. With love I felt balanced. In the end, we're not rewarded for our diplomas, but for our scars.

I even forgave the nurse who had fallen while carrying my two-day-old baby girl, killing her on that hard hospital floor. I felt compassion for her.

I had kept my heart closed a lot because I was afraid to suffer. Now I saw that suffering was a way to feel compassion for the sufferings of others. I was really doing well with staying compassionate and forgiving with clients, friends, family. I made a list of the people I wanted to forgive, like the tobacco companies who seduced me to start smoking when I was twelve, but neglected to tell me that I might not be able to quit when I wanted to. I knew my lungs were severely damaged, and worse, my children were smoking, too. Since I'd smoked during my pregnancies, they were born addicts. I was finding it difficult to feel compassion, or to forgive the companies until they changed their deceptive advertising campaigns. I began writing a letter to a cigarette manufacturer about the need to inform the public of the addictive properties of nicotine, when I heard that a U.S. military plane, carrying nuclear weapons had crashed. Four out of five safety switches failed on impact, leaving us one switch away from bombing ourselves.

I wondered where I'd been for the last fifteen years while the world had been busily preparing to destroy itself. Then I remembered. I had been picketing a paper company for emitting forty times the

legal amount of toxins into the air, threatening an outbreak of
leukemia, cancer, and emphysema. My kids and I wore gas masks,
and along with fifty or more concerned citizens, we handed out a
pamphlet entitled *It's Your Sky, Too!* I was interviewed by the media,
and that night I got a telegram, "If you want your children to stay
alive, keep your nose out of the air." I never protested anything after
that. Crimes against nature and the perils of our planet slipped
through my consciousness as easily as my dreams when I didn't write
them down. I had been blinded and deafened by the prospect of my
children being murdered. I closed my heart to the cries of mother
nature, and remained untouched.

"I'm compassionate and forgiving," I told myself, until I heard
that a friend's sixteen-year-old son had leukemia. They lived one mile
from the plant I had picketed fifteen years before.

I needed to cry. I needed to get rid of the feeling I had in my
belly. It was anything but compassionate or forgiving. It felt like a big
black ball, and I needed to release it. I needed therapy. Therapy is
having a good cry, scream or laugh. It's listening to the wind, watching
a sunset, walking on a beach. It's being listened to, cared about and
understood. Therapy is education, plus love.

I called my friend Sophia, who had endured many sufferings with
me. She was a sister . . . we loved and trusted each other.

I lay on my back. Sophia sat behind my head, holding my hands
and providing resistance for my pull. I began to breathe deeply. Then I
let a long, steady tone come from within. At first, it felt as if the sound
were coming from my belly. Eight or ten tones later, it sounded as if it
came from my toes. I threw my head back (carefully), opened my
mouth as far as I could (comfortably), and screamed. I let go of all the
breath I had, and in that last little force of air that I pushed out . . . I
saw my black ball disappear. I felt it, too.

Then I screamed again. It was like sonic surgery.

I screamed at acid rain, threatening the harmony of nature. I
screamed at the prospect of babies being born with unimaginable
defects, and at the horror of calculating their deaths as a by-product of
nuclear power. I screamed at my fellow humans woven into a web of
elementary evil and blatant stupidity, who could let people starve to
death, while surplus grains rotted in storage. I screamed at the
absurdity of a world threatening to sacrifice its people for nothing,
because if there's a nuclear war, nothing will survive.

I needed to cry. I needed to be held and cradled as I cried for a
people faced with annihilation. For a people who were in the habit of
waiting for their leaders to give them what they had convinced them
they needed. I cried for all the mothers who will have to watch their
children die and at the prospect of my own children's lives pre-
maturely ended . . . for nothing.

When it looked as if I'd cried enough, Sophia stroked my head lovingly and said, "At any given moment, you're either grateful or complaining."

"I don't feel grateful," I said softly, hardly able to talk at all.

Sophia said, "Well then, be grateful you don't have to eat a live frog."

I smiled, "Death may be the biggest event since birth, but unnecessary, premature death pisses me off. As a therapist, can I encourage people to take responsibility for their lives but leave the safety of their air, food and water up to the same assholes who are threatening to blow us up?"

It was Sophia's time to laugh. "Perhaps," she offered, "you could say, 'Well, Mr. Smith, if the world's about to self-destruct, you won't have to worry about whether you hate your mom more than your dad.' "

We laughed together.

"What's it going to take to stop the insanity of nuclear weapons and waste?" I asked despondently.

Sophia, still soft and centered said, "If our love for each other isn't strong enough to save us . . . maybe our terror will."

I breathed deep and said, "I accept that our little planet's in big trouble, even the frogs. . . . I belong on this planet, the earth's my mother. . . . I commit to helping people be peaceful." I was feeling better.

"Brava," Sophia said, and we laughed and laughed and. . . .

BLUE ETHER HEARING

Location :   *throat*

Sound :   *HAM*

Color :   *blue*

Element :   *ether*

Function :   *communication*

Sense :   *hearing*

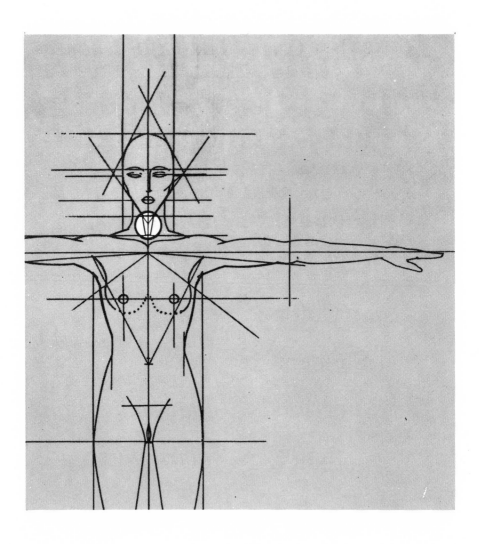

Issues

PHYSIOLOGICAL issues include disorders of the thyroid gland, throat, neck and ears: inadequate voice, stiff neck, sore throat, earache, overly acute hearing, deafness. Balanced physical functioning brings well-regulated metabolism.

EMOTIONAL/BEHAVIORAL issues deal with mis-communication: over-interpretation, poor auditory comprehension, difficulty with self-expression, shyness. Balanced emotional functioning brings skill in singing, dancing, writing, public speaking.

SPIRITUAL issues deal with understanding the truth and healing with harmony.

Questions

- Does anyone understand me?
- How can I make myself heard?
- How can I best express myself?
- Who is there to talk to?
- Who are my friends?
- Am I a healer?
- Can I trust myself?
- What are my commitments?
- Why does it sometimes seem that people talk meaningless babble?

5

Communication

Life Partner Commitment

I give you the most precious gift of all . . .
I give you love.
I give you care and protection.
I commit to encouraging your search for personal
 freedom
And your exploration for truth.
I give you total trust,
Absolute forgiveness
And an open heart.
I give you honesty.
I commit to never betraying or abandoning you,
Or leaving you hurting.
I shall love all other women/men as sisters/brothers.
I take you as my life partner,
As a constant image of God(dess) in woman/man.
I take your hand in friendship and love.

Inner peace, then the world. What was a successful therapist doing naked in a small tree in the wilds of the Amazon twenty-four hours after she'd climbed up there? I was learning tricks to become peaceful. With my heart open, I had begun to hear what it was saying. I was less and less able to listen to the lies of my mind. Once I heard what my heart was saying, it became impossible for me to remain confused. I needed to learn ways of healing.

Signs and symbols popped up everywhere, pointing me towards Peru. I picked up a magazine and there was a Peruvian fertility symbol on the cover. A friend called from Canada, offering me a plane ride to Peru. Late one afternoon, as I sat in my car patiently waiting at a railroad crossing for a passing train, a man hit the back of my car. He jumped out of his car, I jumped out of mine, and he looked as startled as I was. He said nervously in his best but broken English, "Lady, I have no insurance, you take this instead, okay?" With that he stuck a gold Peruvian fertility symbol in my hand, winked, and ran back to his car. When I arrived home, my friend Jack called and said he needed to see me. Jack was a seeker, a visionary, and a mediating lawyer who knew the injustice of the legal system.

He arrived enthusiastically waving an unlikely gift he'd received from an East Texas redneck . . . a Peruvian fertility symbol hanging on a gold chain. Not being people to take signs and symbols too seriously, Jack and I both went to Peru to see what the shamans were up to.

The tricks I learned were not as important as learning that tricks work. The shaman's message is simple: "Give the power to the patient, and let the patient believe in the healer." Each culture has its unique diseases, and shaman do whatever works to help patients activate their own immune systems. But what a Peruvian shaman can get away with in Trujillo, is likely to get her arrested in Texas.

One shaman, Don Ernesto, assisted by his wife and son, used the magical powers of a visionary vine as a sacrament to truth. Twenty of us circled up in a bamboo hut in the jungle, and ceremoniously drank some of the vilest tasting black molasses stuff called Ayahuasca. The hallucinogenic induces visions . . and vomiting. After we had all had a turn or more at the latter, the visions came and came and kept on coming.

A huge sinister black panther stood guarding the door of our hut. I tried to blink her away, but she just sat there, looking serious. I got distracted by an animal who seemed to come in from nowhere, and would have scared Walt Disney. A few animals I'd only seen in comic books sauntered around the room, keeping me spellbound. Everyone in the circle saw the same animals. The ceremony had begun at midnight; now after three or four hours of being subjected to visions that I was afraid would never disappear, and to the relentless bopping on my head of the zen stick held by the shaman's wife, Mata, whenever I tried to use sleep as an escape, I looked over and saw a huge multi-colored parrot, perched on Don Ernesto's shoulder.

"Do you see that parrot?" I asked, poking my friend Jack in his ribs.

"Of course," he said nervously. "Do you?"

We began to giggle nervously when suddenly the parrot hopped down and landed on Mata's shoulder. He began wildly pecking his jagged, hooked, sword-like beak violently into her unsuspecting eyes, nearly poking them out. She struggled, fell to the floor, bleeding from her eyes, her face scratched and torn. I was paralyzed. So was Jack. The black panther lunged toward the woman, and we froze completely. Jack squeezed my hand so hard, it took days for the blood to come back. I squeezed my eyes shut and held my breath.

An hour later, the sun was rising, and so was the shaman's wife. She was bouncing around offering juices, looking as bright as the morning sun, without a mark on her face. What had I seen? I pondered the question for months. So did Jack. But when there are no answers, the questions disappear. Shamans, like most normal people,

offer individual style and expertise. One gifted shaman in a small
Peruvian village, Don Roberto, works with a guinea pig, which he
passes all around the body, then skins alive. He reads its entrails to
diagnose disease. I knew about cat scans, but a pig scan was new to
me.

Don Roberto did ceremonies with San Pedro cactus, a hallucinogenic plant that's also taken as a sacrament for clarity of vision. In
another magic circle, we gathered on a cold and windy Peruvian
beach. We were given a black shell filled with the cactus juice, then we
had to cover the left nostril with the thumb, throw our heads back,
and pour the liquid into our nose. The cactus juice burned going
down.

The shaman whistled a haunting melody while the participants
drank. Then, one at a time, people began to stand in front of him to
ask the one question we were allowed. One man asked, "Can I trust
my business partner?"

"No," came the response. "He is at this very minute driving a
long white car across a long high bridge, where he intends to sell some
stock that belongs to you."

Even in the dark, I could see the man's face turn white. His
partner owned a long white Cadillac, and their bank was in a city a
long, high bridge ride from their office.

It was my turn. I knew, because my friend Jack shoved me into
the middle before I could think about it. I hadn't noticed any effect
from the San Pedro cactus until I walked towards the shaman's mesa,
or altar, filled with varied power objects. Suddenly, a burst of
energy struck me, magnifying the sounds of the gentle breeze into a
whistling hurricane. A pig's grunt reverberated as loud as the roar of a
herd of buffalo. I blinked and a wooden horse on his mesa lifted its
head. A large bouquet of black coral began vibrating. He began slowly
chanting my name, and suddenly I was standing in front of the shaman
but he was a boy of about eleven or twelve. His face was the same,
only younger. He was wearing the same funny little dark blue woolen
cap. His eyes were big, black, wet and mysterious. He was sitting at a
long low table, sculpting a clay bowl.

His mother came to him and said, "Your father's waiting. Hurry."

"I'm not ready," he said flatly.

"Your father will be angry," his mother said.

"My father's in heaven." he said quickly.

I watched with awe as his mother compassionately touched his
shoulder and left. I was stunned. I didn't know whether to go on and
ask my question, or to say what I had seen.

"Do you often see scenes of the past?" Don Roberto asked
through his translator.

Again I was shocked. How did he know what I had just seen?

He asked me to go to someone else in the circle. I went to Jack. He was standing there looking like he'd rather be home. His black beard had a little white icicle hanging from it, and his eyes were shooting stars in the dark. Then . . . he was a child of six or seven. He was standing near his teacher's desk, looking terrified. The teacher picked him up and took him onto her lap, and held him close as the rest of the class looked on. She was about to tell him that his mother had just been killed in an auto wreck. I blinked really hard, and there was Jack, looking like his wonderful, worried self.

"Jack," I almost choked, "was your mother killed in a car crash?" He looked as if I'd hit him, then he reached out and we hugged and cried together.

I never did get to ask my one question which would have been, "Why can't I see scenes from the past when I want to . . . at will?"

Later that night, I remembered Charlie saying, "Seeing the past, like the present and the future, takes practice. We usually get what we prepare for."

I had always seen the future. My timing was off, that's all. When I'd say, "My dad's going to buy me a bicycle," and six months later I was the only kid in the neighborhood without one, it seemed as if my predictions were lies. By the time my dad actually bought the bike, I distrusted my intuition. Because I couldn't see the past whenever I wanted to, I discounted the phenomenon. Now I realized that seeing the past was a gift that helped me understand people's problems. I had to learn to trust my powers if I hoped to inspire trust in the people I worked with.

Most of the shamans I met were healthy, energetic, and loving. They knew Mother Nature, and how to mother nature. They had a deep respect for the elements. The spirit of fire was a living entity, and they used it well. They listened to the wind, used the air to cleanse themselves, and got grateful at the sound of water. Herbs, plants and flowers were seen as global gifts, and they used them to heal the hurts people suffer. They didn't charge money, though they often asked for some. They would never consider not helping someone who could not pay. Never! They only asked what someone could comfortably give. Shamans never lived better than other villagers. They were guided by the spirits of nature.

One shaman I came to know and love, was guided by the spirit of alcohol. Don Julio was purported to be a great healer when he was sober, which was on Sunday mornings, between six and ten. In my very best poor Spanish, I offered him help with his alcoholism. He assured me his spirits were guiding him. I told him I knew the spirit of whiskey, and that I'd like to offer him some choices. In his inimitable way . . . he accepted.

Each day we would sit together and be silent. He taught me how to listen to the wind, and we listened alone, together. In the beginning,

I could only hear the sounds the wind made whizzing by my freezing ears. If ears could chatter, mine would have. Eventually, I began to hear beyond that sound, and it was as if I tuned in a cosmic frequency that sang a universal song.

One afternoon I was sitting with the wind and my alcoholic shaman buddy was sitting beside me. We were perched mid-way up Juanapichu, cloaked in our ponchos and knitted caps. At first, I felt a gentle breeze caressing my face. My eyes had been closed for a long time. Then I sensed the presence of something, or some animal, just to my right. I opened my eyes and saw my friendly, proud eagle perched beside me. Gusts of wind blew through my being then. I began to shiver, and my body felt frozen.

The next thing I knew I was lifted onto the eagle's back, and we soared towards the sky. We were well into the clouds when I looked down at the mountain where I'd been meditating. There I was, still sitting, looking meditative. Don Julio, still sitting beside me, looked depressed.

The eagle flew still higher, when suddenly, without warning, I fell. I began tumbling backwards, like an astronaut somersaulting through space. I landed on my feet, but on a violet-colored plateau, complete with crystal mountains, illuminated by stars that seemed close enough to touch. I was greeted by an incredibly beautiful and completely bald little girl about eleven years old. Her astonishing, florescent eyes smiled as she said lyrically, "Welcome home."

I tried to speak, but there were no words.

"The less we speak, the more we hear," she said. Her voice was like a symphony. "It's easy to speak the same language when we don't use words."

I heard her words though I couldn't see her lips moving. Her message seemed to come from the stars in her eyes.

She recognized my bewilderment and offered, "You'll soon be down to earth, so remember this: harmony is life itself. When it resounds in humans through song and laughter, in the pulse and beat of the heart, it touches the soul. When harmony penetrates your innermost depths, it will create a new life force. The sound of humans in harmony, will bring joy to all existence and lead Earthlings to peace."

Once more she tried to allay my anxiety. She said motheringly, "Many people on Earth already have stars in their eyes."

She hugged me then, and she felt human. I felt fulfilled. I blinked and she was gone.

The next thing I remember, Don Julio was tapping my shoulder, with an ear-to-ear grin covering his face. In his Incan-Spanish dialect he said, "The spirit of alcohol has gone." Then he laughed and added, "Now you go home and find a man with stars in his eyes."

I had stopped asking questions I knew couldn't be answered . . .

peacock

and I was really grateful I didn't have to explain what had happened, because I had no idea myself.

On the plane flying home from Peru, I was listening to my silence and heard, "You're lonely, you jerk. You want a partner in your life. You're horny, and if you want to stay healthy and happy, you'll couple up."

Now that my mind was listening to my heart, I knew it was true. I was as lonely as a slow grey cat accidently left outside in a winter rain.

Sophia was a true friend: we accepted, tolerated and determined not to change each other. When I said, "I want a man in my life," she arranged for me to meet one. He wasn't exactly what I had visualized . . . he was much better looking and considerably younger. I had believed that the man had to be older. Now I know that isn't true.

We knew we loved each other as friends when we both got bored enough at a mental health professionals' meeting to leave together, share a joint and the secrets of our souls. Once I got over my shock from his braces, we got close enough to really make out.

He gallantly lived through my cyclonic love relationship with a close friend across the sea, and even went along with an experiment in triadic living. The nice thing about trying an alternative lifestyle was that when it didn't work, I got to try alternatives. I'd always believed that three in a bed was as unlucky as thirteen, now I knew it. Perhaps, if the two men had been sexually turned on to each other, it might have been less insane, but it was not possible for me to live tri-angularly. Just trying to keep the bizarre relationship between the three of us a secret from the rest of the world, was as impossible as standing on a busy street corner, naked, in the middle of winter . . . unnoticed. There are no secrets in families, people just wish there were. One of us had to go. It could have easily been me. The guys enjoyed each other.

My friend from afar wanted absolute sexual freedom: the priv-ilege of being sexual with many other women. I found I still wanted one life partner: someone with whom I could bond and be committed. My across-the-sea lover was a passionate, hard-core romantic. I knew the fun . . . and also the fragility of romance: it could fade at the first forgotten anniversary, or at the sight of a better pair of legs. It didn't appeal to me to go from playing "please the parents" to "please the partner," or to worry about being left like yesterday's pasta . . . cold and sticky.

I wanted someone who shared my aspirations for inner peace, and was dedicated to cultivating his spiritual life as much as I was . . . preferably someone who liked cold spaghetti for breakfast. My Texas friend did. He even practiced kundalini yoga. He wanted a partner so much, he'd been reciting a mantra every day for seven months for marriage with a beautiful, spiritual wife . . . preferably someone with a cute ass and plenty of money. We were both ready to consciously commit to increasing our psycho/sexual/spiritual capacities. We both loved loving.

He moved into my house as quietly as he had entered my heart. We didn't even have to rearrange the furniture.

I wasn't lonely anymore.

I began doing workshops and taught people tri-energetics: kundalini yoga, bioenergetics, shamanic healing, and how to celebrate sound and silence. In five days people made progress they could not have made in six months or a year of weekly individual therapy. I knew the magic of a healing circle, and I knew that if I could cultivate my psychic talents, so could everyone else.

I found that people who came to my workshops were people like me searching for a lot of love, a few good laughs, and a little peace.

Once we got beyond culture, people were the same. We'd all been taught to repress our feelings and our sounds. Many of us had been imprisoned in over-crowded classrooms and squeezed into miniature desks, where we were forbidden to talk, much less scream. The sounds people made were the same the world over. So were the problems they shared. Releasing pent-up sounds made it possible for people to hear each other as human beings, all suffering the wounds left by people who did the best they could.

It took being among people gathered like a family, without our stereotyped sex roles, to experience the miracle of being an ordinary normal human being. That's all it took. As soon as people stopped being afraid of each other, stopped saying nasty things behind each other's backs, we felt safe enough to be free and loving. Once we believed in each other's powers, we had them. We empowered one another.

People brought their partners, parents, children, and forgave each other past mistakes. Some people left the workshop with a whole new and more satisfied feeling about themselves and others.

We sang, danced, made music, played theatre, discovered hidden talents, had ceremonies, did yoga, formed new and meaningful relationships, laughed, cried, shared, and acknowledged our individual, personal powers and despair. It didn't take a course in miracles to learn to expect one.

As people broke through their walls of defense and denial, as they began to release their negative spirits, they experienced relief in the form of inner peace. But the better they felt, the sicker I got.

Often, after workshops, it would take two or three weeks of periodic fevers, depressions, anxiety and acting out the symptoms of people I'd worked with, for me to get back to normal.

I had one difficult experience with a stubborn spirit who followed me across the sea, and who had me looking as though I could have an epileptic seizure at any moment. After that I decided to go to a world gathering of shamans and find out what was happening. Spiritists, herbalists, shamans, tricksters, healers of the highest kind, mad-women and crazy ladies, wizards, witches, masters and phonies, all gathered to share information, expertise and love. Standing under the bright Austrian sun, sipping tea with an unforgettable-looking East Indian shamaness with long black hair and a tall black lover, I learned part of the answer.

"You're a psychic sponge," she said brightly.

"What's a psychic sponge?" I asked, trying to act sophisticated and intelligent.

"A psychic sponge is an ordinary person who heals by opening herself up enough to eliminate all resistance to everything."

"That's me," I said gleefully, blowing my cool. "I'd know myself anywhere."

Now I can consciously decide to school myself in the art of psychic sponging. After all, who wants to be a spiritual garbage collector, exposed to unimaginable misplaced, restless, psychic slime that sometimes lingers in the sponge?

I went to talk to a North American shaman who had a reputation for knowing about protection. He wouldn't let me come near him because I was menstruating. He was protecting himself. I was out-raged.

I gathered a group of women to discuss our periods. For the first time in my life, I celebrated my bitchiness. For the first time ever, I was proud of my period. I left that circle appreciating the menstruat-ing woman . . . and the spirit she embodies.

When I left that conference I knew that I couldn't change the way I worked, but I could choose who worked with me.

My beloved met me at the airport with the news: my father was dying.

I'd never spent a lot of private time with my dad; my mother didn't encourage it. Now I was suddenly free to take him to the country, to some of the wonderful little places I knew in the woods . . . and talk, read and really commune with him.

First, we denied that he had less than a month to live. Then we got angry. Then we bargained for more time, got depressed . . . and finally we both accepted his fate.

We tried every non-invasive remedy from herbs to Interferon, but six weeks after he'd been diagnosed, he was lying in a hospital bed unconscious, and hours from death.

I was standing at his bedside . . . teary, sad, reconciled. He was, naturally, incontinent. I knew that he needed to urinate, I'd been watching the nurses handling him for two weeks. There was no nurse around. I reached down and got the bedside urinal, took his penis in my hand, holding it so he could pee. In that instant I became free of culture, conditioning and religious thinking. I experienced my father without judgement, criticism or projection.

"Oh God, I love you Daddy!" I said, still holding his penis. I loved him absolutely and unconditionally.

I put the urinal on the floor, pulled the sheet up to his neck to cover his cold shoulders . . . and wept. I cried tears I'd been saving for a lifetime. They spilled down my face and soaked my sweatshirt.

"Daddy don't go yet, I love you!" I heard myself sobbing. "I know you didn't understand me . . . but I know you always loved me."

I cried for all daughters who ached for the approval of their fathers, and for every father who was too afraid of his own sexuality to allow the physical closeness that heals the hurts between parent and child. I cried for every father who never knew his children, and for those who wished they hadn't. I cried for all fathers who did the best they could, and who in the end never knew if they had made it. I cried for all the little girls who learn too late the futility of being their father's daughter. I cried for all fathers who die before they can forgive themselves. . . . I put my face against his and he was gone.

My mother's death came eighteen months after my father's, and wasn't any easier. She and I had spent years doing battle. We clashed at every corner. We caused each other immeasurable anguish and we always came back for more.

My mother was someone I couldn't live with, and couldn't leave either. She had the ability to reduce me to an angry infant with one raised eyebrow.

I couldn't believe the pain in my heart was so strong two days before she died, that I found myself screaming into her almost totally deaf ears, "Please don't die before you let me love you! Please let me love you!" The nurses were moved to sobs, but my mother remained stoically analytic.

I never fully understood my mother. On her last day in a very darkened hospital room, she complained that it was too bright. I was confused. She'd always prided herself on her ability to complain without smiling, and somehow she managed to stay in character to the bitter end. As I frantically struggled with a hospital blanket to block any last remnant of light from coming through the window . . . she died.

Her last words were, "It's too bright in here!" Leave it to my mother to complain about the *light* with her last breath.

I looked at her face. For the first time in my life I saw her smile a smile that could have healed the world. I took her hand in mine and wondered if she would spend her next life in love and laughter.

Beyond the grief and pain of the loss of my parents came a sense of freedom. I felt freed from the burden of my past, and of the cumulative wisdom of the ages. I became an individual, unique and total.

Now that I had time to really notice who I was living with, I turned my attention to the beloved friend who had nursed my parents as if they were his own . . . and had sustained me with his love and laughter. I felt grateful, but more . . . I felt at peace.

It's hard to notice things when they're staring us in the face. Luckily, I saw that here . . . in my very own house, sleeping in my bed and squeezing my toothpaste . . . was my protector . . . the finest ghost-buster around.

He knew all about psychic protection . . . how to use crystals, gems, precious metals and mantras. One thing about psychic phenomena is that the results are clear . . . like shamanism, it either works or it doesn't. There is no diploma testifying to your qualifications. What you do that works earns you your degree. As soon as we began working together, I stopped getting sick.

We were married in a flower-flooded temple by Sant Keshavadas, a singing minstrel who had been teaching my lover how to heal with mantras as well as how to manifest a wife with one. In our lovely white robes and flower garlands, we took the seven steps in a traditional Hindu ceremony, just like the Gandhis, and I promised, "I shall be as a sister with all other men."

The impact of that vow didn't hit me until two days later, when a man I wanted as a friend began flirting. I told him the conditions of a relationship with me: no hanky-panky.

He dropped the "me-man . . . you-woman" game, and related to me as a person. I had always loved being around loving people, even men . . . but usually sexuality, or the fear of it, prevents men and women from knowing each other. Now I could have all the brothers and sisters I wanted. Knowing I was safe let men come closer to me. Even married people need friends . . . and a lack of interesting diverse relationships results in clandestine affairs. My commitment set me free.

At our second wedding (I'd always believed I could have only one per husband) my two luscious daughters and his two beautiful sons danced and skipped down the aisle of our Unitarian Church. My sister's son led fifty of our closest friends in a hand-clapping, foot-stomping sing-along. As my sister's song-spirit daughter opened everyone's heart with her healing voice, I walked slowly and proudly down the aisle beside my beloved dog Shiloh, who still had a grin on her face.

INDIGO SIXTH SENSE

Location: *third eye*

Sound: *OM*

Color: *indigo*

Element: _____

Function: *intuition*

Sense: *sixth sense*

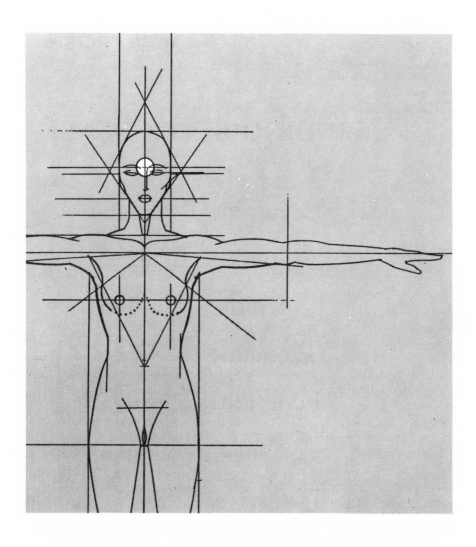

Issues

PHYSIOLOGICAL issues include distortions in vision, headaches and insomnia. Balanced physical functioning lets you focus the mind, stop thinking and rest when necessary.

EMOTIONAL/BEHAVIORAL issues deal with integration of intuitive awareness: knowing without data (paraperception, extra-sensory perception), excessive thinking, control of thoughts, original thought. Phenomena that may become a concern include pre-cognition (knowing the future), prophetic dream visions, clairaudience (hearing sounds not present), clairvoyance (seeing things happening elsewhere), psychometry (knowing the history of something by touching or seeing it), telepathy (mind reading), telemention (influencing others with thoughts). Emotional imbalance can result in severe thought disorder, delusions, hallucinations, autistic thinking. Balanced emotional functioning draws on a wealth of information not available to the five senses.

SPIRITUAL issues deal with integration of super-normal powers. When the energy of the brow center takes on the vibration of any of the five lower chakras, its own vibration is lowered and is influenced by the emotions. Balanced spiritual functioning can beam the light of pure thought into the senses and help harmonize the discords of life. The more free the mind becomes from the lower chakras, the more self-contained it becomes in its own vibration. The ability to concentrate the mind and set it free allows us to beam the light of intuition up to awaken the highest consciousness.

Questions

- Am I psychic?
- What do my dreams mean?
- Why do I think so much?
- What about time and space?
- Are there extra-terrestrials among us?
- Can spiritual lovemaking liberate me?
- What happens when time stands still?
- Can I see the past, present or future?
- Can I read minds?
- What's it all about?

6

Intuition

To Free Thinkers

I honor those who dare to think new.
Bravo to those intuitive few
Who know they must take a positive stand
So Earth won't become No-Woman's Land.

It's a good thing the world doesn't have to be at peace for me to be peaceful, because I know the world will not get there before I do. I don't need anyone to tell me that, it's one of those things I know all by myself. Just like when I "knew" that even though my parents told me they were buying me a kitten because they loved me, it was really because we had mice in the attic. I knew if I wanted to inspire people to live life like a song, I'd have a lot more people singing along if I learned to stay in harmony.

I'd begun sleeping under the stars on the front porch of our little rented Galveston beach house that overlooked the Gulf of Mexico. One morning just before the sun came up, my husband began brewing coffee, and I watched the waves wash in an ocean of garbage . . . orange peels, broken bottles, beer cans, old holey socks, soggy TV dinner wrappers, light bulbs, and occasional unidentified flying objects, all compliments of the off-shore oil rigs.

I sat calmly as we sipped our coffee, and listened quietly as he explained that the site of the new hospital where he was to work as a medical psychologist, was directly across the street from a highly contaminated toxic waste dump.

I propped my feet up on the porch rail and nonchalantly turned my head just in time to see a man come tearing out of our neighbor's house, having just robbed it. We listened to the harmonics of the award-winning burglar alarm waking the dead, and my husband called the cops, a bit reluctantly, too, knowing they were bored with the same old complaints.

As we waited for them to arrive, trying to hear each other over the ear-buster alarm, my secretary (who'd been up all night) phoned to tell me that she had learned that the alcoholic I'd been seeing (who was in such bad shape I wondered how he managed to drive to my office) wasn't unemployed . . . he was working as an air traffic controller at the local airport.

I listened to the shrill screaming burglar alarm, got up, took a deep breath, and screamed . . . in perfect harmony.

I liked Texas. It was what was happening to it that inspired me to move. But where? We began mentally shopping for a country we might like better than the USA, and considered the criteria. First, it was most important to never move to a country that didn't let you leave. Next, we wanted to live somewhere where our tax money didn't pay for nuclear weapons that would either destroy us on purpose, or by accident. We wanted to live without radioactive toxic waste in our soup. We preferred a nice, quiet place in nature where the trees were still unafraid of the rain, and where we could encourage people to take a deep breath without being afraid the air would kill them. We wanted to live somewhere where loving peace didn't make us subversive . . . somewhere where peace-making was not unpatriotic.

Patriotism brought up the same feelings I had when my mother would say, "It doesn't matter whether I'm right or not, I'm your mother . . . so I'm right." Patriotism, like organized religion, was like making love with the wrong person: it only worked if I kept my eyes closed. I'd tried keeping my eyes closed. I hadn't read a newspaper in twenty years, and I knew as much about politics as I did about the private fantasies of the Pope. Still, I knew great billion dollar underground shelters were planned and about to be built, to house politicians and papers after a nuclear attack, and that meant the United States had some crazy idea they could win a nuclear war. They were certainly preparing for one . . . and we get what we prepare for! I'd known there was no utopia, now I knew there was nowhere to hide.

When I began working around the world, I developed a sense of planetary patriotism, and knew that moving around wouldn't be a problem because my family and friends would visit and Charlie would find me anywhere.

"Who's Charlie?" a woman in a workshop in Austria asked as we walked among some ancient pines.

I was speechless. Language is linear, Charlie's round. I breathed, remembering as if it were yesterday, that first time I'd met Charlie.

My skinny, hairless, eleven-year-old legs trembled as I stretched them along the cool mattress of the upper berth of a swift train to Texas. I snuggled under the sweet-smelling sheet. The giant train began slowly thrusting forward, then rocked and swayed and shook me like a cradle in the sky. Back and forth, round and round, the train lulled me, played its whistle for me, and thrilled me with its speed. Relaxed, I let the rocking, swaying motion soothe my spirit. I closed my eyes, and let my fingers rest on my little mound of peach fuzz. Soon I was fondling myself, absorbed in the hypnotic rhythms, sounds and sweet smells. I played and rocked and swayed with the motion of the giant, slick, swift train. As it screamed and screeched and thrust, I fondled faster and faster, carried by the rhythm of the universe. I felt safe, I knew heaven was on earth, I loved life. I let go. As the giant train's whistle screamed through my ears, I screamed a giant, silent scream into my pillow, "Oh God, Oh God!" . . . and there was God.

For lack of experience and more creativity, I managed to intuit God in the body of a short, light-brown man with starry eyes and a belly like Santa Claus. I named him Charlie.

I answered my friend's question with, "Charlie is a little man with a big belly."

I never could explain Charlie to anyone but my sister. I tried to make my parents understand, but my mother got so worried she made me swear I'd never touch myself again, and my father not only refused to listen, but stopped looking me in the eyes after that.

My intuition, along with my sexuality, free will and original thought, was anything but encouraged. Most of us have had trouble with our intuition. Like sex, it was never taught anywhere. I'm not complaining. It wasn't too long ago that big guys with little understanding called intuitive woman "witches" and burned them. I only got ridiculed, "Don't be ridiculous, people will think you're really weird," or threatened, "If you ever lie to us like that again, you'll wish you hadn't."

I scared my parents to death with comments like, "Oh look, there's the green lady," or "Here comes the purple boy."

Luckily, I had my sister. It was through her I learned that "weird" was wonderful, and meant that I was on my own path to my personal destiny. She saw people in color, too. She was enough older than me to be a surrogate mother. She filled in the blanks for nurturance and good humor, and she comprehended the paranormal. We'd talk endlessly without words. We knew when the other was having a great time, or was in trouble. After she moved from home, we'd write each other letters and then read them, as best we could, before opening the envelope. Distance brought us closer. Instead of playing "Let's pretend" like other kids, we played "Let's predict." We predicted everything from which of our children would lose the next tooth, to the damage from a predictable hurricane. With my sister I belonged. She encouraged my faith in knowing that some day I would meet a man as weird as I was, and we'd be terrific together.

At one point she was my entire support system, my lifeline, and I was hanging on by my fingernails.

That's when she died. I had not seen Charlie for many years. Usually, I would have to be lost in my Self, for Charlie to appear. Now, I was standing at my sister's funeral with her two sons and daughter, surrounded by people I didn't understand and didn't want to, consumed with sadness at the thought of her children growing up without her, and wondering how I would manage without her, myself.

Then Charlie showed up. "When the need is greatest, the guru appears," Charlie said tenderly . . . and I projected everything I had, and was, and ever hoped to be, onto that consciousness. At that moment I knew I would be with my sister again.

It wasn't until I was standing in a pizzeria, holding my pizza-to-go with one hand, and trying to pay for it with the other, and a man came in waving a gun and demanding the money from the cash register, and I stood calmly watching as the thief backed out of the door with the money in one hand and my pizza in the other, that I realized I could count on Charlie.

Perhaps it was because I grew up in a city where the grass was covered with concrete, the flowers were plastic, and nature scenes were murals in Chinese restaurants, that I needed a guide like Charlie. I was a child of technology, not of nature. There were only two trees in the park near my house, and one of them needed to be in intensive care. Nature spirits of wind, water, earth and fire were as foreign to me as take-out pizza was to a shaman in Peru.

The spirits of animals, on the other hand, were my friends. As a child, stray cats and dogs followed me home regularly, and at a zoo I could communicate with the animals better than I could with the people who brought me. For years, I have enjoyed the spirit of a great-looking proud eagle, who still shows up when I need her, and a great gorgeous lioness who plays as gently as a lamb.

Once during a workshop, we were all holding hands and chanting, "OM . . . OM . . . OM." We were doing a fire ceremony under the stars and bright full moon, and the theme of the workshop had been "Fly like an eagle." Just as we were about to stop the chant, a huge bird, looking more like an eagle than an eagle, flew into a nearby tree. Everyone was speechless. Once we try to explain the supernatural, it ceases being spiritual, and becomes technology.

During another workshop, when I was wondering what to do about a very young, and big burly bear of a man who was a little afraid of my lion (my lioness is always around me when I work), I asked Charlie, "What does a lioness do to help a bear feel better with her?" I turned around, and there on the wall, facing me, was a painting of a lion . . . dancing with a bear. I turned back, stretched out my arms and the young man came into them . . . and we began a frolicking, fun-filled dance and a life-long friendship.

Now, sandwiched between two majestic white pines in the midst of the Austrian Alps, I didn't need any intermediaries to know that the trees were dying. All I had to do was look. What I could have used were a few suggestions for what to do about it. Intuition is more than knowing what was, or what will be; it's a matter of accepting what *is*.

During that Austrian workshop, a woman brought her six-year-old child who was retarded. She came wanting a miracle . . . a cure for her son. As she lay on a mattress, surrounded and supported by the group, she screamed, "Why me? Why me? Why me?" until her screams could be heard forever. Then the miracle happened. She got the answer and we all knew the exact instant she got it. She got that there was no answer. She intuited the truth, and in that moment, she accepted it. When next she hugged her child, she wasn't wishing he could be different, she was loving him as he was. She didn't need anyone to tell her that her son would never be normal, anymore than I needed anyone to tell me that I could get close to God during orgasm.

I trusted my intuition and knew that I never got more spiritual or peaceful, than after (or while) making love. I knew that it was as impossible to jump up immediately after a total orgasm feeling terrible, as it was to run out and joyously bomb people I loved. I knew that "Make love, not war" had been retired to the graveyard for dead dogma before we'd had a chance to learn *how*. Making love instead of war seemed intelligent.

I imagined what would happen if the military got it and changed their games, toys, and costumes. Commissaries would feature bedroom boutiques, and Captain Cox would design naughty nighties for sexy soldiers. The military could lead the world in high-fashion sexual accessories. To satisfy a need to compete, they would hold an International Military Olympic Games spectacular, and amuse themselves with such electrifying events as plane-flying-low-enough-to-scare-the-hell-out-of-people, but not-low-enough-to-hurt-anybody. The military would evolve into an elite corps of skilled specialists, heaven-sent to lovingly restore health and balance to our ailing planet.

It seemed to me the military, like politicians and normal people everywhere, were suffering from closed hearts, boredom and dead sex. The difference between the predictable violence that erupts from bored, frustrated, love-starved civilians and from the heads of states, is the number of people who can't get out of their way.

It seemed to me the only couples whose relationship thrived were those with a spiritual base, not a religious one. I knew spiritual didn't exclude sexual. The tantric and Taoist approaches to spiritual sexuality appealed to me. When I heard they emphasized the need for a man to keep the woman absolutely satisfied, I said, "Sign me up!" I wanted to become an adept. Luckily, my husband did too. He even stayed committed after learning that he would have to regulate his orgasms, and not have an ejaculation every time we had sex.

We started off slowly, going to every available workshop, buying all the books written about it, and setting aside time we didn't have, to practice.

Our first tantra course paid off. I'd worked for years learning to like my genitals, but I still had a hard time knowing what to call them. Now, instead of a pussy, I had a *yoni,* and I could have a *jade garden,* or a lovely *lotus,* if I chose. His cock became a *lingam,* a *magic scepter,* a *healing wand,* or when I was feeling especially grateful, a *jewel.* Just singing *OM MANE PADME HUM,* the jewel is in the lotus, was a turn-on.

One night, in the height of passion, he nearly strangled his sacred staff trying not to come. He whispered huskily through gritted teeth, "This is not going to work, this is going to kill me."

We held each other tenderly, he settled down, and I whispered, "Have you noticed your hair recently?" We took a break . . . I had always believed making love was like riding a train: once you got on the right track, you kept going. He looked in the mirror. His bald spot was sprouting. Baby hairs covered a small but significant patch of his head. We ran back to bed and started over. Now, instead of wanting to give up the whole idea of regulating his emissions, he was a born-again *Tao of Loving* practitioner . . . and more committed than ever to mastering the art.

What we were practicing was working. He'd begun regulating his orgasms and didn't come any more often than the Tao suggested. Apparently, all that semen had to go somewhere; it went straight to his head and his hair grew! Not only that, but as an extra bonus for doing his homework, he was able to make love whenever he wanted to. It was, however, the concept of his ultimately being able to have orgasms without ejaculating, that kept him practicing. I'll never forget his first success. We celebrated in a bubble-bath (I always believed men hated baths), and affectionately christened his lingam Long Time Sun.

The more I trusted my intuition, the more my beliefs changed. I'd believed I had to be in the mood for love. When my husband suggested we begin to cultivate the habit of sharing love every day, I was appalled. It takes forty days to form a habit, and I was in the habit of getting into the mood when conditions were right: when I wasn't too tired, too pensive, too interested in other things; when I wasn't too anxious about having to get up early, too full, too close to my period, on my period, too gassy or if I hadn't just eaten onions. "I'll give it a try," I said half-heartedly, hoping he'd forget about the plan. Three years later, daily love-sharing (though not always sexual) had become a spiritual practice that was not only growing in intensity, but was keeping our spirits up . . . and our weight down. Instead of disciplining ourselves to work out every day, we made out every day. Questions like, "Will he want to? . . . Is it too late tonight? . . . Am I in the mood? . . . Didn't we just do it last night? . . . Do I want to?" . . . all disappeared.

As a reward for all those years of keeping up with kundalini yoga, we went straight to the head of the red tantra class. White tantra had taught us how to channel our sexual energy, and now we got to channel it straight to bed. Some yoga postures were more fun when we did them together, some became really spiritual: a gateway to God often opened when he tended the jade garden and ate the fruit of the womb.

The nice thing about practicing control over the body is that getting older really does mean getting better.

I had always believed that I took too long to get turned on. Now I knew most women take a lot longer than men, and it was important to explore ways to harmonize so that he wasn't boiling over, waiting for me to warm up. We both knew the healing power of touch, and we used that power to relax each other, to help release stress, sounds, and pent-up emotions. We massaged, did double yoga stretches, and discovered that by consciously practicing the many different ways to touch, we could reach perfect harmony.

We practiced singing in harmony, and even hummed the same note into each other's mouths. That's how I discovered the art of kissing. I'd always liked kissing, but I never thought it was a big deal. Now, we practiced everything from passing delicate drops of wine back and forth with our kisses, to his sucking on that sacred sex spot right there in the center of my upper lip, to stimulate my clitoris. I'll never know how I managed to live half my life without knowing it was there! I stopped taking kissing for granted, and started taking it for all it was worth.

I began to see how harmony heals, in more ways than one. By harmonizing our posture, rhythms, sounds, and even our bodies' juices, we were balancing our hormones and found we could cure the common cold. I had a hard time imagining myself explaining this stuff to my mother-in-law, however, when she'd telephoned complaining of a cold, "Just lie on your right side and let Dad thrust into you a hundred and eight times tonight, Mom, and you'll be over that cold by morning."

We dallied in our discoveries. We languidly titillated and tantalized each other with promises, caresses and fantasies. We fantasized everything from his having several sweet young girls with bobby socks, and bows in their braids, to my being restrained in silk ropes, while one by one, twenty men took me as he played with himself . . . and watched, of course.

When we began fantasizing with consciousness, we developed the ability to prolong periods of ecstasy. My tolerance for pleasure increased dramatically, but I still enjoyed the freedom to get distracted and inspired enough to jump up in the middle and write a poem. Through successive heights of ecstasy, we began to see visions with our minds, feel them with our hearts, and even dream them simultaneously. Yoga had prepared us individually for what we were experiencing together.

We visualized the world being free and loving. Each day people everywhere would spend one minute in peace, and consequently, the world was peaceful. We visualized the rich and famous demanding peace, knowing that the rich and famous usually get what they want.

Once during a tantra workshop, we were familiarizing ourselves with the G-spot, that magical power source living right inside the jade garden. The weather was hot and sultry; sun streaked through our little private, flower-filled room. I was lying on my back, naked, propped up on three fluffy pillows. My beloved was kneeling comfortably in front of me. We looked into each other's eyes, silently touching. We had been asked not to let ourselves become sexually aroused during this exercise, but to remain concentrated on staying aware and in touch with what was going on with each other.

He'd been gently yet firmly massaging the inside of my thighs, relaxing them, letting me release some stress. He was letting the love from his heart flow out of his hands, so with every touch I was safer, warmer and more responsive. Our gaze was so strongly connected, it was as if we were joined at the eyes, and I wondered if it would hurt when we separated them. Holding the gaze, he slowly began inserting his middle and index fingers inside me. My legs gradually opened just wide enough to provide him access to my inner self. Still holding my eyes, he began to feel around inside me until he found the G-spot with his fingers. He used his other hand to press firmly, just below my belly. As he massaged the spot, I felt a slight irritation, as if I wanted to urinate . . . and then it subsided. I told him how it was feeling (we had expected it), and he stayed right there skillfully, gently, persistently moving his fingers around.

I kept going deeper and deeper into his eyes, until I went beyond the stars. I began to see images of life-time, of love-times gone by.

I was a little girl, a wild mischievous sad little girl. I was lonely, isolated, separated from the source, from my real mother.

I saw myself tumbling backwards through time and space, twirling and struggling to hold the silver cord that kept me connected to the stars.

"Who am I? Where do I come from and where do I dare to go? I'm a child of chance, ripped from the skin that could save me, by the greed of those who lied." I heard myself whisper, "No more lies! Please, oh please, stop the incessant lies we whisper everywhere. Now . . . I want more of *now!* Now I feel truth. Now . . . I want more of now."

"Now, in this moment," I thought, "I accept myself . . . and now, here, I accept this man who has come so close to my soul . . . he's joined it."

I breathed, opened still wider, trusted. I belonged with this twin soul who knows how to reach the source of creation. That's when the heat began to travel up my spine. Bursts and rushes of heat rose with my breath, and I began to shiver.

He took his hand from my belly and covered my chest with my scarf. "Breathe," he encouraged. "Stay connected."

I breathed, opened wider, looked deeper. I was a witch, an intuitive woman who knew what the truth was . . . and wanted some. I was a witch who knew we must together love our way to new ideas.

"Love a witch," I played. "What do you have to lose?"

He smiled wide. "Witches conjure what they want through their sacred will and manifest what they know is right."

"I want to manifest a safe place for our children to live. I want to help create a world safe enough for human life to survive," I said without thinking.

"Hang on, heat waves," I thought. "I'm still safe here with my beloved and my sisters and brothers. Faith is the past . . . hope, the future. Witches don't have faith or hope. . . . We make things happen."

He fondled and caressed my sacred spot, and I was a wild, wonderful, crazy lady . . . my father's daughter? . . . perhaps the daughter of a thousand shining stars . . . the star stuff the crazy ladies wear with big-brimmed hats and shoes too high and nails of Chinese red . . . a crazy lady who, beneath the makeup, is still the *Shakti,* the potent female energy that can change the face of the Earth . . . whose yoni is the portal to the past and the future, a sanctuary for incarnating souls, a pleasure field of heaven, a sweet and beautiful flower, complete with perfume and nectar, surely worthy of being worshipped and kissed.

I opened wider, relaxed even more, breathed. . . . I let the heat rise and the tears fall. I saw his tears, too.

He was such a little boy, with trees and tractors, screaming his fears into the night with only his mother's verses for solace. He was a wizard, a magician turning grey, dead promises into dazzling diamond words. He was a holy man: an ordinary man who keeps his commitments. He was a saint. Oh yes, a saint, who took the pain of the planet to his bosom and soothed it with noble intentions.

I thanked the stars then for all little girls, witches and crazy ladies . . . and for all little boys, wizards and holy men. I didn't need anyone to tell me I was a goddess. . . . I knew it! A goddess is an ordinary woman when somebody loves her. A goddess is an ordinary woman who's found her soul.

When he released his hand, we embraced and sobbed together. I felt so beautiful . . . so absolutely spectacularly holy . . . like such a gorgeous goddess, I could have run out of the room shouting, "Hey! Look at me! Look what I have between my legs! Isn't it amazing!"

Luckily, I didn't. Instead, we hugged and laughed and celebrated the privilege of knowing each other so deep . . . so unafraid.

I saw all women in a different light after that . . . and all men, too. Now I knew that people are perfect, it's the world that's crazy.

VIOLET CROWN

Location: *crown of head*

Sound: *SOHAM*

Color: *violet*

Element: ____

Function: *cosmic connection*

Sense: ____

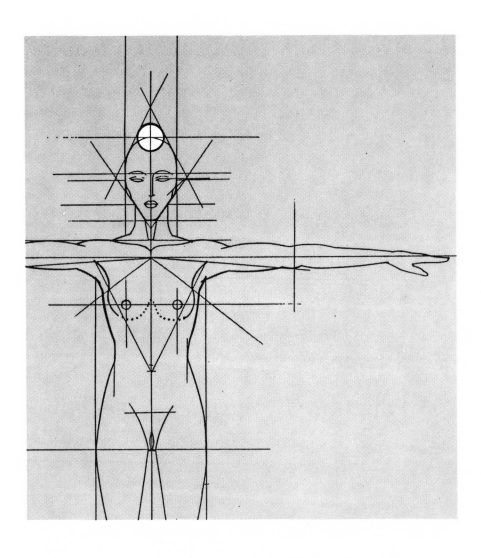

Issues

PHYSIOLOGICAL issues include headaches, insomnia, hot and cold flashes, discoloration and swelling of chakra regions, sensitivity to light, chest and back pain, dizziness, loss of appetite for sex or food or much of anything. Balanced physical functioning enables life to go on despite the above conditions.

EMOTIONAL/BEHAVIORAL issues involve detachment and bliss. They may bring loss of ego-investment and freedom from selfish desires.

SPIRITUAL issues center around being at-one-with Divine Light, Cosmic Intelligence, The Absolute . . . and often involve selfless service.

Questions

- Who am I not?
- If I am that I am, then who are you?
- Do I want to reach a state where I stop getting angry, being judgmental or turned-on?
- Do I desire freedom from desires, passion or responsibility?
- Would I enjoy ignoring children, not feeding birds or never arguing?
- Would it be fun to stop dancing or singing, remaining detached from the sounds of this world?
- What's the difference between enlightenment and death?
- Why am I here? Is it worthwhile to remain?
- What form will I take next lifetime?

7

Cosmic Connection

On Enlightenment

*Once I believed in religion's metaphysical fairy tales.
They seduced me to explore enlightenment's possible
rewards. It was defined as ambiguously as possible,
and seemed to be reserved exclusively for men. Still
. . . I yearned for freedom. I wanted cosmic consciousness, detachment, bliss.*

*I became cautious when enlightenment began to sound
more like death than awakening. It was beyond acceptance, belonging or commitment . . . above gratitude,
love, caring, forgiveness, communing or cooperation.
After lifetimes of suffering, starvation and sex depriva-
tion, and after mastering such feats as jumping rope
without ever touching the ground, being rewarded with
egolessness left nobody to celebrate the victory. It was
like promising a prisoner the electric chair as reward
for good behavior.*

*When I got off my knees, crossed my legs, and began
counting my breaths instead of my money . . . I
discovered moments of transcendence. These exquisite
occasions were sparked when I was in the overwhelming depths of nature, when I was near death, when I
had taken a consciousness-altering sacrament, or
when I was in the rapture of love and transcended the
duality of flesh and spirit.*

*There are as many definitions of enlightenment, cosmic
consciousness, liberation, awakening, as there are
ways to get there.*

*For me, cosmic consciousness is oneness with life, and
being inspired to selfless service and moral action.*

Liberation is the freedom to tolerate, change or be grateful. It is the freedom to protect and preserve this planet and her people from annihilation.

Awakening means being consumed with awareness of the present. It means dropping denial and accepting what is. It means giving up beliefs in exchange for knowing.

Enlightenment means living in the light of truth. It doesn't mean knowing everything. To me, it means knowing we can either light-up when we destroy ourselves, or when we see the stars in each other's eyes.

That choice is our destiny.

I was an ordinary cosmic law-abiding goddess, looking for a lot of love, a few good laughs, and a little peace. I had learned ways to feel better, safer and happier, but being free and loving had become a full-time job.

During workshops, alone in nature or being intimate, I could be free and loving. It was natural. Out in the world of shopping centers, auto repair shops and five o'clock traffic, it wasn't so easy. Normal people are unaccustomed to being hugged before being introduced.

I determined to act free even when I felt about as free as a fly trying to swim out of a bowl of chicken soup. I knew it was easier to act my way into a new way of feeling, than to feel my way into a new way of acting. I acted free. I gave away all my possessions, so I wouldn't be possessed by insurance companies. I stopped answering the phone just because it was ringing. I ordered my pizza with the cheese on the side. I wore my hair like a lioness and my clothes for comfort. I told myself I was free. I started to talk less, and spent several hours a week in silence. I stopped living up to other people's expectations. I began telling the truth. I didn't care to be any richer than I already was, because I knew that success in the material world meant having my statue standing in some park with pigeon shit on my nose. I realized that freedom really did mean having nothing left to lose. I knew that I didn't have to answer every question I was asked. . . . That's when I was arrested.

Luckily, I knew that whenever I was supposed to feel guilty it was a set-up, because I had stopped doing things that brought me guilt. The details of the arrest are as irrelevant as the fact that all the charges were dropped. But the twenty-four hours in a small, cold cell gave me a fresh new look at freedom. When I was released, I wasn't acting free . . . I felt free. I know I'm free when I feel free. How could I aspire to something I'd never fully understood?

My partner and I celebrated that the good guys always win with a tantric ceremony. Ritual had become a way to experiment with our inner lives.

We stood silent in the sunrise, feeling grateful. We did some peaceful, playful yoga, stretching away the weariness and invigorating ourselves, and went in search of affordable flowers, some new white candles, and hypnotic incense. We bought nuts and berries, some exotic cheese and rare wine. We scored a loaf of fresh French bread, and this year's apples.

While standing and waiting our turn to pay for the apples, I felt an impatient tugging on my pants leg. I squatted down, and stared into the luminous, star-lit eyes of an angelic-looking toddler who appeared out of nowhere.

"You have stars in your eyes," she said smiling.

"You do too," I said, barely able to get the words out. Her face was identical to the bald-headed child I had seen in Peru.

Just then her mother came and scooped her up into her arms. Before the mother could leave, the child reached out and kissed my cheek.

"Thank you," I said nervously, shaken by the baby girl's words and face. "Want to tell me something else?"

"Oh," her mother said quickly, "she hasn't started to talk yet."

I knew there are no accidents, and that every event and incident was a direct message from somewhere, I just didn't know where. It took hours to recover from the shock.

We began our ceremony at home with my lover suggesting we bathe under a water-fall. We did. We splashed and sprayed and meditated until the shower turned cold. When we stepped out, we began to dry each other by tongue, but it got too cold, and we huddled under our king-size towel, and made our way to our room.

It looked like a temple. The altar was adorned with happy yellow-faced flowers, and bright-burning candles that illuminated pictures of our loved ones. A single long-stemmed rose, my symbol for protection, reminded us that we could experience the mystical union with the universe when we felt love for other human beings.

We stood naked in front of the altar, just looking into each other's eyes. Then we took a comfortable tantra seat, and gazed long and deep into each other's eyes. Gradually, we began to synchronize our breathing. He'd breathe in, and I'd breathe out. It was like giving and getting, simultaneously.

He began stroking my hair, and then spontaneously, he got up and took some sandalwood oil from the altar. Sensually, he massaged my hair and scalp with the oil, and I felt cared for, adored. He brushed my hair as I ached to have it brushed when I was little . . . without pain, just pleasure. I sat quietly, reveling in the feeling of love that each stroke of the brush brought.

Then, when he stopped, I massaged his hair and scalp and neck with the oil. I played with his head the way I used to play with my children's, and the way it felt best when I had it shampooed . . . first gently, then in circles, then harder, then faster, and slow again. He looked transfixed and dreamy-eyed with the pleasure he was feeling.

We sat in our tantra seat again, our right hands pressed against each other's heart center, and began to harmonize our chakras by chanting the vibrations that opened and balanced them. We chanted until we were vibrating in tune with each other.

Then he took my hands in his, pressed them against his heart, and kissed my fingers, sucking them one by one, and scraping his teeth across the length of each finger. I relaxed down to the sheep skin mat and lay on the floor, filled with joy and anticipation. He kissed my eyes, oh so sweetly; his lips played with my lashes, his tongue told my eyelids they were loved. He kissed my cold nose, and I smiled and he kissed my wet teeth.

"You're a banquet," he said, "a smorgasbord of heavenly tid-bits and delectable delights." I play swooned. He continued, "My mouth waters at the sight and smell of you," and I lapped up his loving language.

He rolled me over, and began alternately massaging and sucking my spine. He massaged, sucked, licked, massaged, sucked . . . and the waves began to flood me. He whispered his breath deep into my ears, sending shivers up my already electrified spine.

The back of my neck became the center of his universe. He sucked and kissed and bit and played and whispered unhearable words of gibberish into my whole being, right through the back of my neck.

"Ohohohohooooooooooooooo," I said.

Then I was on my back, looking straight into his endless eyes. He spread my legs apart, as if they belonged to him, and I surrendered, knowing they did. He caressed the inside of my thigh first with his warm hands, then with the side of his face, and then by rolling his head around between my thighs, then with his cheek, and his nose, and mouth and beard and tongue. He stretched out then, and had me lie on top of him. I grasped his toes with mine and held them tight, turning and twisting and making little adjustments so I could feel as much of his supple, super body against mine as possible. Our bellies caressed each other.

Oh the blending, the silken, spinning and weaving of magic threads of togetherness . . . oh, the silliness, the playful, innocent merry-making.

I couldn't seem to prevent myself from reaching for his lingam, it looked so lovely and full of promise. I cupped his scrotum with my hand, and began to lick the length of his phallus with my tongue. Before I could indulge myself, he said softly, "Stand up, my goddess."

Suddenly, I was standing there in front of the altar, naked, smiling, and feeling very silly.

"Let me make worship on you, and sanctify our spirits," he said, sounding serious. I covered my giggle with a fake cough, and my embarrassment by closing my eyes.

The next thing I knew, he was standing in front of me, looking like a skinny Santa Claus, with a grey beard and stars in his eyes. He adorned me with a graceful flowing turquoise belt I'd never seen before. It encircled my hips and provocatively framed my yoni.

"Wow," I exclaimed before thinking. Then, I felt so gauche, I over-compensated and said, "What a lovely gift to bestow upon me on this auspicious occasion." I stood tall and proud and so undeniably happy.

Then, he was on his knees in front of me. He looked up and into my eyes, then to my feet and began repeating words we had learned as ritual.

"Blessed be thy feet, that have brought thee in this way." And he kissed my feet.

Then he kissed my knees and said, "Blessed be thy knees, that shall kneel for what is holy to thee." I breathed and listened.

"Blessed by thy womb, without which we should not be," and he kissed my yoni as sweetly as if it were a baby's mouth.

"Blessed be thy breasts, formed in strength and beauty."

"Oh God," I thought, "I'm feeling it now."

Finally he lightly kissed my lips and said, "Blessed be thy lips, that shall speak about truth, trust and love."

Just as I was about to switch places and recite the ritual to him, he stopped me.

"Let me go again," he whispered. "This time, I'll do it my way."

He got to his knees again. I stood there looking holy and goddess-like in my new exotic belt. He took my right foot to his mouth, and slowly began sucking my big toe. Luckily, I could stand on one leg as easily as two.

"I bless these feet and this crooked toe," he said, "with all my heart because they walk the path of universal understanding and love, and they walk that path beside me."

I sighed; I was loving it.

"I kiss these knees," he said smiling, "because even if you think they're too fat and funny, they are bold and proud, and only bend for the truth, which sometimes includes my lucky lingam."

I was having a good time now.

He kissed my pubis with about ten rapid "I love you" kisses, and said, "Blessed be this most sacred gift, this haven, this home, where I am forever finding limitless delights and endless bliss."

My whole body began to smile.

Then, kissing my breasts in turn, he said, "Blessed be these sweet breasts, that let me feel safe and sound when I suck them, loved and nurtured when I rest upon them, and turn me on whenever I notice them peeking unexpectedly out of a thin silk blouse."

I laughed . . . he laughed . . . and then, kissing my lips he murmured, "I love this mouth of yours, and want to kiss and lick and suck the sweet truth that saturates us both when you open it." He kissed my mouth again, and then, looking into my eyes he said, "I love who I am when I see myself in your starry eyes."

Oh, how we hugged . . . our nakedness felt like a fur coat. We slid to the sheepskin and spread ourselves out in unabashed, uninhibited abandon.

That's when the door bell rang.

"Don't get up," he said good naturedly, "or you'll never know the heights of unexcelled bliss you will have missed."

"I have to trust my intuition," I said, putting on my clothes, but secretly thinking that I was free enough to ignore a ringing phone, but not free enough to let the door bell ring.

The man who had rented my parent's house was standing at the door.

"I found this box of letters in the attic," he said, "and thought it looked important enough to hand deliver."

He was right. He handed me a box of letters from Lenore . . . my sister.

I wandered back to our bedroom sanctuary and sat in awe of the shoe box on the floor.

There in front of me, filled with her premonitions, promises and poems, were the letters I knew existed, but had never seen. They were chock-full of private predictions and magic messages that echoed from the weather-worn, almost withered pages.

I was so grateful at finally finding them, I didn't care that my mother had hidden them for over twenty-five years. I leaned against my beloved, and he held and supported me as I opened the first envelope.

For my sister with the stars in her eyes,

Once upon a time, a goddess was born.

She didn't know she was a goddess, because nobody ever told her she was. She was taught that gods and goddesses, like shamans, witches and wizards, were either mythical characters, or too holy to emulate.

During her life she discovered her own ideas, and came to know that the world was nothing but ideas. She learned the art of causing

*change in consciousness by acts of sacred will. She knew the
necessity of training the will and imagination, because reality is a
function of the level of consciousness which perceives it.*

*She was a dream-weaving goddess who spun a web connecting
hearts and minds in oneness with Mother Nature, herself.*

*She knew the healing power of love, and she inspired people to
peace, because she believed the good guys will win, and she was a
personal friend of Santa Claus.*

*At her funeral, her loved ones noticed a short brown man with
stars in his eyes, but only a few saw the eagle perched on his
shoulder, or the lion at his feet.*

First Chakra Exercises

1 *Deep Breath*

Breath is the life force, the flow of energy between the poles of spirit and matter. As we breathe, so we live. Besides, no breath . . . death!

INSTRUCTIONS: Inhale through your nostrils, filling your belly with air, letting it expand . . . hold on . . . bring the air up to the lungs and let them expand. Hold your breath . . . exhale slowly with control . . . contract your belly, pulling it towards your spine. Leave the breath out until you have to breathe again . . . through the nostrils. Repeat the whole process.

If you want to change your breathing habits: take one deep breath . . .

> at every traffic light,
> before answering the phone,
> before starting to eat,
> before going through a door,
> before standing up,
> when nobody's looking.

Wear a button that says "Breathe" on it.

2 *Grounding Posture*

Life is a matter of breath and posture. When you stand straight it allows the energy to move freely up and down the chakras.

INSTRUCTIONS: Stand naked in front of a mirror. Tell yourself you love what you see, even if what you see isn't even close to what you'd like to see. Align your body starting with the feet. Point the toes in slightly. Bend your knees slightly (stiff knees are a popular way to stop energy). Relax the buttocks. Let the arms hang naturally. Relax the shoulders . . . down. Relax the head to see if it's aligned evenly on the shoulders. Do what it takes to really feel grounded . . . put both feet firmly on the ground, and inhale as if you are getting the breath through your feet.

3 *Make a List*

Listing our issues helps to clarify them.

INSTRUCTIONS: Simply make a list of things you fear, things that worry you, things you'd like to have, things that are important for your survival. When you have completed the list, select those items you would like to release and bury them at least six inches underground (earth is the element for this chakra).

4 *Archer Pose*

This posture is powerful for increasing self-confidence and the ability to cope. It focuses the mind, grounds the body, reduces anxiety . . . and . . . it makes you strong and graceful.

INSTRUCTIONS: Stand with your right leg bent forward enough so you can't see your toes over your knee. The feet are about one meter apart. Your left leg is straight back with the foot flat on the floor at a forty-five degree angle to the front foot. Raise the right arm straight out in front, parallel to the floor. Now, make a fist as if grasping a bow. Your right thumb is pointing straight up. Pull your left arm back as if pulling a bowstring back to your shoulder. Create a tension across your chest.

Breathe long and slow. Concentrate on one point, either on the horizon, or on your thumb. On the inhale, silently say "SAT" (truth). As you exhale, silently say "NAM" (the name).

To increase intuition, focus your attention at your brow center.

To begin, do two or three minutes per leg. Let yourself increase your holding time, but listen to your body. Relax on your back and totally let go of all your stress, worries, anxieties.

Archer Pose

5 *Temper Tantrum*

This is an exercise that can be done at home, preferably while someone you know and trust assists you.

INSTRUCTIONS: Lie down on a bed, a mattress on the floor, or on lots of soft cushions so you won't hurt your heels or hands.

Take lots of deep and rapid breaths. Let out a loud sound. Make fists and raise your arms and legs. Alternately hit and kick while screaming. Just scream out whatever comes to you.

After you have released enough emotion (trust yourself), it's nice to have someone comfort you. It helps to lie in your partner's arms or lap and let yourself be held for a few minutes. A feeling of deep relaxation almost always follows a temper tantrum. So does a good laugh.

One good laugh is worth a week of tears.

6 *Star Gaze*

This shamanic exercise *works!*

INSTRUCTIONS: Sit yourself comfortably in front of a candle-lit mirror. Breathe some long, slow, deep breaths. Look into the lights in your eyes. Watch them become stars. Let those stars allay your fears.

Second Chakra
Exercises

1 *Seven Chakra Sex*

When we understand the chakras, it's easy to see why there's frustration, anxiety and emptiness in sexual encounters of the lower kind. To be satisfying, sex must involve the heart, spontaneous expression and communion, intuition, and the wisdom of the soul. It must include spirit . . . to matter.

When a woman submits to sex for money or from fear, or because she's afraid to be alone, or if a wife or husband succumbs to obligation, or a man just needs a port in a storm, or needs to satisfy his basic biological needs (like masturbating, only into a woman) . . . it's first chakra survival sex.

When two people are drawn together through lust, desire, or because they imagine the other to be the lover they've been waiting for . . . they're having second chakra sex.

When a need to control, manipulate, or get even with someone is the turn-on . . . it's third chakra stuff.

When people come together with love, respect, care and friendship and want to please each other sexually . . . it's a fourth chakra encounter.

The fifth chakra may let your soul dance as you hear the songs two loving hearts sing.

In the sixth you may intuit, smell, taste, see, touch, and know the God and Goddess in your partner. You may sanctify your souls through your sexuality . . . and intuit the truth.

Seventh heaven.

Sat Kriya

2 *Sat Kriya*

This exercise works directly on stimulating and channeling sexual energy, allowing you to utilize it for healing and creative activities. It is excellent for general health maintenance and disease prevention. It massages the internal organs, keeps the body in maximum condition, and activates all levels of consciousness. It should be practiced for at least three minutes daily, for optimal results. It is helpful to begin with three minutes, rest for a minute or two, and begin again with another three minutes, until you have done the kriya for a total of fifteen minutes, and rested for eight or ten. I have done Sat Kriya for up to thirty-one minutes . . . and thrived. Please don't push yourself so hard that you miss the subtle experiences of energy inherent in this kriya. A kriya is an exercise that involves a series of energy relationships among different chakras. Prepare yourself slowly, and reap the rewards . . . on all levels.

INSTRUCTIONS: Sit on the heels and stretch the arms over the head so that the elbows hug the ears. Interlock all the fingers except the index fingers which point straight up. Chant "SAT" (out loud) from the navel point and solar plexus, pulling the navel in to the spine. Chant "NAM" as you relax the navel. Keep the chin slightly tucked in, the spine straight, the arms straight up, and the rhythm at about eight *SAT NAM*s every ten seconds.

When you end, inhale and squeeze the Moohl Band (root lock) by tightening the muscles of the anus, sex organs and navel point. With your eyes closed feel the energy moving up the spine. Exhale, holding the lock . . . squeeze even tighter. Inhale deep . . . hold tight. Exhale and relax.

3 *Getting Balanced*

INSTRUCTIONS: When you put on your socks in the morning, instead of leaning against something or sitting down, stand up and practice balancing yourself on one leg. Don't get discouraged if you fall over at first. With persistence it works. Whenever possible stand on one leg, (especially while standing in line). Eat one complete meal with the unused hand . . . sign your name, brush your teeth and hair with it, too.

4 *Make a List*

Not everyone likes to write. But lists help us reflect on our behavior . . . so well, that most people enjoy making them. You can make a list of anything in your life that interests you . . . a guilt list, a belief list, a turn-on list, a habit list, a list of favorite-gifts-I-have-received, a things-that-make-me-nervous list, a my-favorite-excuses . . . the list is endless. Intelligence is limited by awareness. It's intelligent to become aware of our behavior. The best way to balance our chakras is to become aware of them.

INSTRUCTIONS: Take pad, pencil, pen to a comfortable writing place. Take some deep breaths and decide what list you'd like to create. Give yourself fifteen minutes, and write whatever comes into your mind about the subject.

If you share a list with a friend, you're more likely to do something about it than if you keep it to yourself. Share your list as openly as possible for anywhere from fifteen minutes to several hours.

Then ceremoniously release whatever no longer serves your noble intentions . . . into a body of water (the element of the second chakra).

A river or ocean is a superb place to let go. . . . A toilet will do.

Third Chakra Exercises

1 *Pounding Pillows*

There are three most efficient ways of letting go of anger and all include sounding-off: have a temper tantrum (First Chakra Exercise), have a good scream (Fourth Chakra Text), or pound some pillows. This simple exercise helps prevent violence because it allows expression of anger and aggression. Children love it!

INSTRUCTIONS: Get on your knees on the floor. Be comfortable. Kneel over a pillow that will resonate when you hit it. Raise your arms over your head and make fists of your hands. Breathe deeply about eight times every ten seconds until you can smash your fists against the pillow. Continuously raise your arms in the air and bring your fists down hard on the pillow. Shout, scream loudly.

Mostly people scream appropriate things like, "I hate you. . . . Why did you do that . . . Why did you do that to me? . . . Leave me alone! . . . Fuck you! . . . Don't touch me . . . I'll always hate you . . . I won't . . . No more . . . Why me? . . . Never."

Don't stop too soon. It usually takes two minutes or more to really get going. If you're not aware of buried anger when you begin this exercise, simply act angry. It's easier to act our way into a new way of feeling, than to feel our way into a new way of acting. Pretending anger often triggers the real thing. Many people are prevented from expressing anger or rage as children. Then as grownups, we're afraid to let it go. If we want to get peaceful, we have to get rid of the garbage.

After you've released enough emotion, trust yourself to know when to stop, you can enjoy the feeling of deep relaxation and peace. If you feel so, it's nice to share what you experienced with someone else.

2 *Breath of Fire*

Breath of Fire can: clean the blood, help overcome addictions, prevent shaky nerves, help focus the mind, strengthen the nervous system, increase ability to concentrate, increase physical endurance and stamina, produce a global alpha rhythm in the brain, stimulate and balance energy in the third chakra, release toxins from lungs, mucus lining and cells.

INSTRUCTIONS: The breath is fairly rapid, two to three breaths per second. Breathing is continuous and powerful, with no pause between the inhale and exhale. When you exhale, push the air out by pulling in the abdomen and navel point. Keep the chest moderately relaxed, focusing the energy at the navel point. As you inhale, relax the abdomen, let the diaphragm extend down, and the breath will come in as part of relaxation rather than as effort.

As you do Breath of Fire, remember to relax tension that may build in your legs, face, shoulders, and chest. At first, the navel point and solar plexus may feel tired or uncoordinated. With practice, the breath will become rhythmic and very easy.

Once you are practiced, it's possible to do the breath for twenty minutes or more, without dizziness or imbalance of oxygen in the blood. Old toxins and deposits from drugs, smoking, food additives, etc. are released through the blood and lymph systems. If you're very toxic, Breath of Fire may stimulate a very temporary self-toxification. To aid the cleansing process, increase the amount of exercise you do each day, simplify your diet to fruits, vegetables, and nuts, and drink plenty of water.

In most exercises Breath of Fire is done for three minutes or less. As an exercise by itself, you can start with three minutes and slowly build-up to twenty.

To perfect Breath of Fire, keep the spine straight, the chin slightly tucked, and your mind centered. It helps to mentally vibrate *SAT NAM* with each breath. Hearing this sound tells your mind what to do with all the energy you generate.

3 *Body Sculpt*

For a fun and fascinating experience of being molded by someone, try this with a partner.

INSTRUCTIONS: One person stands totally passive. If you're comfortable being nude, that's fine. The other person begins to place the arms, hands, fingers, head, feet, etc. as if the person being moved was a mannequin.

When you're being sculpted, relax and breathe normally . . . remaining completely passive. Keep your eyes unfocused. Enjoy what it feels like to be sculpted, moved, manipulated.

When you're sculpting, keep changing the facial expression and the whole body until you like the finished pose.

The sculpted partner holds the pose for a full minute . . . to five minutes . . . or more.

Sculpt the person into a posture that exaggerates her life issues (Take care of me . . . I need help . . . I stand on my own . . . Why am I so fat? . . . etc.)

Sculpt the person so that he stands perfectly straight and balanced.

As a gift of love sculpt the person into a posture that is the most graceful, balanced, beautiful one for her.

4 *Stretch Pose*

This exercise activates and balances the energy of the third chakra, sets the navel point, tones the abdominal muscles, and increases your ability to keep commitments.

INSTRUCTIONS: Lie on your back with the legs together. Pointing the toes, raise your heels six inches. Stretch the arms out straight pointing at the toes, and raise your head and shoulders six inches. Focus your eyes on your toes, and begin Breath of Fire. Continue for one to three minutes.

At the end inhale, tighten the muscles of the anus, genitals, and belly. Hold . . . squeeze . . . and relax.

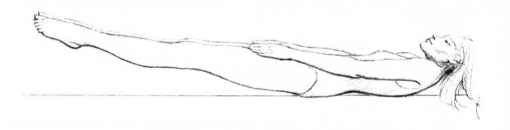

Stretch Pose

5 *Make a List*

INSTRUCTIONS: Make a list of any of your third chakra issues:

People I'm angry at . . .,

I feel powerful when I . . .,

Being successful means. . . .

After you've made your list . . . have a little ceremony, and burn whatever no longer serves your noble intentions . . . and prevents you from getting on with new issues. Fire is the element of the third chakra.

Fourth Chakra
Exercises

1 *Bear Grip at Heart*

This exercise opens the heart and stimulates the thymus gland, mission control of the immune system.

INSTRUCTIONS: Sit on your heels. Place the hands in Bear Grip, fingers cupped and interlocked, at chest level with the forearms parallel to the ground. Inhale. Hold the breath and without separating the hands, try to pull the hands apart. Apply your maximum force. Exhale. Inhale and pull again. Continue for one to three minutes. Exhale and relax.

Let yourself completely surrender to the ground beneath you. Visualize whatever helps you to feel compassion, devotion and love.

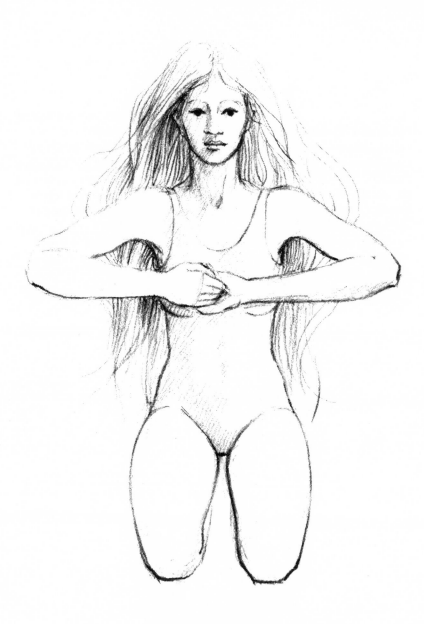

Bear Grip at Heart

2 *Devotion*

It's been my experience that people who have been unfulfilled by organized religions, still hunger to worship. The act of worshiping, though a turn-off to many people, is generally misunderstood, and can bring deep peace.

INSTRUCTIONS: Create an altar (a designated spot in your environment for the purpose of worship), and place something that has special meaning to you on it (a loved-one's ring, a photo, a grandchild's hair). Connecting with this external symbol can help you reach the Godliness, holiness, pure white light, absolute love and/or whatever you most revere.

An altar can provide you with a focal point from which to see your spiritual self. A candle can be a symbol for The Light.

3 *Love a Plant*

INSTRUCTIONS: Buy a new-born plant, and care for her daily with total awareness. Name her. Watch how and what you feed her. Notice the plant's posture, smell, taste, size, color, growth, feel. Touch her, listen to her sounds and think about what this plant gives you.

This also works with big plants . . . like a tree.

The same exercise can be done with a pet, an animal we see now and then, or a power animal (the animal that guides us and is most like us).

This exercise also works with people.

4 *Make a List*

INSTRUCTIONS: Make a list of the issues of your heart. Let go the issues that no longer serve your noble intentions . . . let them fly away in the air (the element of the fourth chakra).

5 *Sing a Song*

INSTRUCTIONS: Arrange for a group of people to gather for the express purpose of singing together. Heartfelt/devotional songs can open hearts.

Solo singing in the car, shower, nature, doing dishes . . . can soothe.

Sing along with uplifting music you enjoy.

Rewrite your favorite hymns with lyrics that support your spiritual growth.

Fifth Chakra Exercises

1 *Neck Roll*

This exercise stabilizes the thyroid gland and balances the fifth chakra. It's great for loosening stiff necks, increasing sensitivity to sound, and relaxing the nervous system.

INSTRUCTIONS: Sit in a comfortable cross-legged position (easy pose). Relax the hands onto the knees. Place the fingers in Gyan Mudra (tips of thumb and index finger touching, the other fingers pointed straight). Begin rolling the neck clockwise in a circular motion, bringing the right ear toward the right shoulder, then the back of the head toward to back of the neck, then the left ear toward to left shoulder, and the chin toward the chest. Inhale through the first half of the roll, and exhale as the chin comes slowly toward the chest. Keep the shoulders relaxed and let the neck be stretched as much as feels good-and-stretched. Enjoyment is guaranteed if done correctly. Continue for one or two minutes, then reverse direction and continue for one or two minutes more. As you stop, bring the head straight until it's balanced on the shoulders. Relax and breathe. . . . Feel what you've done for yourself.

2 *About Menstruation*

This exercise is for everybody, because everybody is affected by menstruation.

Nature's brilliant biological mechanism, menstruation (and the days before it), has been declared a disorder by the medical community. Consequently, millions of women are frantically trying to find a cure for it. There is a better way.

INSTRUCTIONS: Listen to your body. More than likely, it's asking you to give it some nurturing. Stop giving, and let yourself be cared for. Indulge yourself. Some women need to be massaged, others crave privacy.

Celebrate your bitchiness . . . it's nature's protection for you and those around you. Becoming friends with your negativity gives you more energy to rejuvenate.

Seek the company of other women, especially to discuss biological issues, health and safety. Gather in circles whenever possible.

Make love if you want to. Don't if you don't.

If you menstruate or if you live with a menstruating woman, it is helpful to keep a calendar and track the cycle. Preparing for the days when a woman needs special consideration can turn PMS into "Pamper My Self," "Provide Myself Space," "Promise Myself Surprises." When it's your partner's cycle you're tracking, you might mark your calendar, "Pamper My Sweetheart." The Taoists call the first day of menstruation "The Day of the Red Snow."

Avoid looking in the mirror, shopping for fitted clothes, and making life-altering decisions. Avoid salt and red meat. Do not do any hard physical work, or lift anything you can't eat. Do exercise on a regular basis.

Do eat ginger root, green chilies, and cayenne pepper. Do consume complex carbohydrates, quality proteins, and adequate B-complex vitamins. A Chinese power herb called Tang Kuei or Dong Quai (Radix Angelicae Sinensis) is a superb tonic for women, and a good one for men. It brings harmony to the female organs and endocrinology.

The next time you bound from bed in the middle of the night to rearrange the furniture, the next time you feel so irritable you wonder how anyone could love you, or perhaps during your next pre-menstrual eating binge . . . just remember to celebrate the Goddess, through whose bleeding the world goes on.

3 *Listen to Music*

This exercise can prepare you for perfection.

INSTRUCTIONS: Listen to the most wonderful music you can find. Listen to it totally.

You can create limitless ways to entertain, educate and expand your consciousness through listening.

4 *Make a Commitment*

A commitment is a noble intention. Don't make commitments you cannot keep. Most of us are not used to making commitments that we are committed to keeping. Mostly, we make vague promises. We can trust ourselves when we do what we say we'll do.

"I will help you move on Saturday, friend," is a commitment. Unless you die on Saturday, be there and help your friend move.

INSTRUCTIONS: Start small. Be specific.

Write down your commitments so you know to whom and to what are you committed.

Keeping commitments means living the song we sing. Living the song we sing means living life like a song.

Seven Chakra Harmony

5 *Seven Chakra Harmony*

INSTRUCTIONS: Sit in a comfortable tantra seat as illustrated, with your right hands pressed against each other's heart center (you can hold the heart from the front or from the back). Silently, lovingly look deep into each other's eyes and breathe together.

Take a deep breath, squeeze the muscles of the anus, and together sing out "LAM," until all the breath is gone.

Inhale deep, squeeze the muscles of the genitals, and sing out "VAM," until all the breath is gone.

Inhale deep, squeeze the muscles of the belly, and chant "RAM," until all the breath is gone.

Inhale deep, consciously open the heart while chanting "YAM."

With a deep inhale, tighten the throat and chant "HAM."

Then tighten the muscles of the forehead at the third eye, and chant "OM" with the full breath.

Finally, chant "SOHAM," while visualizing the crown of the head illuminated in bright white light.

Repeat the series three to seven times until you feel a balanced vibration between you and your partner.

Note: *a* is pronounced as in *banana, o* is pronounced as in *open.*

Sixth Chakra Exercises

1 *Developing Intuition*

The more we trust our intuition, the stronger it gets. Practice makes possible.

Activity at the sixth chakra, whether intuitive or not, is intelligence. Unfortunately, being stuck at the sixth chakra is almost as confining as being stuck at one of the lower chakras.

Generally, paraperception is spontaneous and cannot be controlled or activated at will. Alcohol, depressives or soporifics reduce ESP, as does stormy weather, skepticism or fatigue. Extra-sensory perception is strongest between people who know each other well and between blood relatives. It is also higher in people living close to nature, and in those who have lost one or more of the five senses. Children and animals often have profound paraperception faculties.

INSTRUCTIONS: These tri-energetic exercises harmonize all the senses, elements and emotions. The good news is that you can do anything you like to knock yourself out at the beginning of the exercise. For example, jump rope, jog in place, do intense kundalini yoga, dance wildly. . . .

When you're exhausted and sweaty, sit cross-legged, keeping your spine straight, chin tucked slightly. Then do one of the following.

THIRD EYE MEDITATION: Let the eyes close and focus as if you were looking from the inside of your head into the third eye point. Press the index fingers over the eyes, with gentle firm pressure on the upper nasal portion of the eye sockets. Press the thumbs over the little flaps on the ears, and close the ear opening. Breathe long and deep. Chant "OM" silently with inhale and exhale, focusing the mind on the third eye. If images help you, visualize a ring of golden light around a blue eye, with a silver star in its center.

CANDLE MEDITATION: Let the eyes focus on the very center of a candle flame. Silently chant "OM" on inhale and exhale. Feel one with the light of the candle.

STAR MEDITATION: Let the eyes focus on a star. Silently chant "OM" on inhale and exhale. Feel one with the light of the star.

THOUGHT TRANSMISSION: Let the eyes close and focus as if you were looking from the inside of your head into the third point . . . and transmit a thought to someone else. This exercise can be done at a specific time at which you have arranged to receive a message as well as to transmit one.

Bibliography:
Books That Inspire

Berne, Eric. *Games People Play.* 1978. Ballantine.

Donahue, Phil. *The Human Animal.* 1985. Simon & Schuster.

Douglas, Nik & Slinger, Penny. *Sexual Secrets, the Alchemy of Ecstasy.* 1979. Inner Traditions.

Dychtwald, Ken. *Bodymind.* 1977. Tarcher.

Girdano, Daniel A. & Everly, George S. *Controlling Stress and Tension: A Holistic Approach,* 1979. Prentice-Hall.

Hamel, Peter Michael. *Through Music to the Self: How to Appreciate and Experience Music Anew.* 1976. Compton.

Khalsa, M.S.S. Gurucharan Singh Khalsa (ed.). *Kundalini Yoga Sadhana Guidelines.* 1978. K.R.I., 800 N. Park Ave., Suite 5, Pomona, CA 91768.

Keshavadas, Satguru Sant. *Healing Techniques of the Holy East.* 1980. Temple of Cosmic Religion, 174 Santa Clara Avenue, Oakland, CA 94610.

Krippner, Stanley. *Psychoenergetic Systems: Interaction of Consciousness, Energy & Matter.* 1979. Gordon & Breach.

Lowen, Alexander. *Bioenergetics.* 1976. Penguin.

Leonard, George. *The Transformation.* 1972. Tarcher.

Macy, Joanna. *Despair and Personal Power in the Nuclear Age.* 1983. New Society.

Millman, Dan. *Way of the Peaceful Warrior: A Book that Changes Lives.* 1984. H. J. Kramer.

Namikoshi, Toru. *Shiatsu + Stretching.* 1985. Japan Publications.

Radha, Swami Sivananda. *Kundalini Yoga for the West.* 1981. Shambhala.

Shutdown! Nuclear Power on Trial. 1979. The Book Publishing Co., 156 Drakes Lane, Summertown, TN 38483.

Shuttle, Penelope & Redgrove, Peter. *The Wise Wound: Menstruation & Everywoman.* 1986. Paladin.

Starhawk. *Dreaming the Dark: Magic, Sex & Politics.* 1982. Beacon Press.

Walker, Barbara G. *The Crone: Woman of Age, Wisdom, and Power.* 1985. Harper & Row.

Wells, Clarke. *Sunshine and Rain at Once.* 1981. Skinner House.

Yogananda, Paramahansa. *Autobiography of a Yogi.* 1981. Self-Realization Fellowship.

Bibliography:
Music That Inspires

Alsop, Peter. *Draw the Line*. 1980 Flying Fish Music.

Armaitischolten, Jetty. *Sufi Songs*. Zuider Buiten. Spaarne 156. 2012 AE Haarlem, Netherlands.

French, Frank. *The New World*. Humanics New Age, P.O. Box 7447, Atlanta, GA 30309 USA.

Freedman, Cindy. *Gift of Love*. P.O. Box 66566, Houston, Texas 77006 USA.

Grigg, Ray, *The Tao of Relationships*. Humanics New Age, P.O. Box 7447, Atlanta, GA 30309 USA.

Heider, John. *The Tao of Leadership*. Humanics New Age, P.O. Box 7447, Atlanta, GA 30309 USA.

Keshavadas, Satguru Sant. *Cosmic Healing Mantras*. Temple of Cosmic Religion, 174 Santa Clara Ave., Oakland, CA 94610 USA.

Khalsa, Hari Singh. *Many Will Be Shaken*. Khalsa Music, 1117 Jackson, Houston, Texas 77006 USA.

Ley, Adano. *Prismer of Love, Vols. I, II, III*. 5127 Richmond #109, Houston, Texas 77056 USA.

Paul Winter Consort. *Concert for the Earth*. Living Music Records, Inc., 65 G Gate Road, Sausalito, CA 94965 USA.

Richter, Otto. *Down to Earth*. Postfach 1311, 7800 Freiburg, W. Germany.

Schiffman, David. *Sounds of Big Sur*. Humanics New Age, P.O. Box 7447, Atlanta, GA 30309 USA.

Sophia. *Journey Into Love*. P.O. Box 1207, Carmel Vally, CA 93924 USA.

About The Author

After a succession of diverse careers, Rickie Moore received a Ph.D. in psychology, and was licensed as a professional counselor. She was a staff psychologist for years, then began traveling extensively seeking to integrate spiritual, psychic and psychotherapeutic approaches to healing. After seventeen years of kundalini yoga practice and years of study with shamans, gurus, teachers and healers, she has become an inspirational therapist with an enormous bag of tricks.

She currently orchestrates workshops around the world, lovingly empowering people to intuit their own destinies in the intensive *Inner Peace Playshop.* Together with her husband, a clinical psychologist, she helps couples strengthen their relationships by increasing their spiritual-sexual satisfaction in *Spiritual Partnership* workshops.

Rickie and her husband live as planetary citizens, dividing their time among six countries. She is the mother of two grown daughters, step-mother of two small sons, and grandmother of two identical baby goddesses. She can be contacted through the publisher, Humanics New Age, P.O. Box 7447, Atlanta, Georgia 30309, (404) 874-2176.

Other New Books From Humanics New Age

For Couples Only
Billie S. Ables, Ph.D.

Most couples fight, but most don't really know why they do. Every relationship has hidden "rules" unconsciously established by the partners. Until these rules are understood the conflicts will continue. Dr. Ables shows how couples tend to act with their partners as they did with their parents. **For Couples Only** gives straightforward strategies for enhancing awareness of you and your mate.

Life Trek: The Odyssey of Adult Development
John Stockmyer, M.S. and Robert Williams, Ph.D.

Life Trek is a chronological journey for the reader through the stages and patterns of adult life from 18-80—and beyond. Based on the latest research, and original contributions by the authors, the book blends historical fables with traditional psychology to point out the timeless nature of the many challenges that affect people throughout each decade of life. Two innovative simulation games are included, giving the reader the exciting opportunity to "play out" his or her own life. The **Life Trek** games even permit the reader to play the life of someone completely different.

The Tao of Relationships
Ray Grigg

The Tao is said to be one yang and one yin in dynamic balance. The balancing of man and woman is not just their coming together, but also their staying separate. The process is two contradictory things happening at the same time. The difference and sameness of man and woman must be simultaneously maintained. Maintaining the paradox is the mystic's art and the lover's art. This is the contention of **The Tao of Relationships.**

The art is practiced by balancing the physical with the mental, the primal with the cultivated, the wanton with the aesthetic. **The Tao of Relationships** is about this balancing and achieving the "extra-ordinary ordinary."

These books and other Humanics New Age publications are available from booksellers or from Humanics New Age, P.O. Box 7447, Atlanta, Georgia 30309, 1-800-874-8844. Call or write for your free copy of our publications brochure.

TM

Trade Paperbacks
For the Future . . . And Beyond

HUMANICS NEW AGE